ISLAM AND THE CONFLUENCE OF RELIGIONS IN UGANDA

1840~1966

AAR STUDIES IN RELIGION

Number Six

ISLAM AND THE CONFLUENCE OF RELIGIONS IN UGANDA 1840~1966

by

NOEL KING

UNIVERSITY OF CALIFORNIA, SANTA CRUZ

ABDU KASOZI

UNIVERSITY OF CALIFORNIA, SANTA CRUZ

ARYE ODED

TEL AVIV UNIVERSITY

Tallahassee, Florida

American Academy of Religion

1973

Library of Congress Catalog Card Number: 73-85593
ISBN Number: 0-88420-105-8

COMPOSED IN PRESS ROMAN TYPE AT THE CSR EXECUTIVE OFFICE
PRINTED IN THE UNITED STATES OF AMERICA
PRINTING DEPARTMENT, UNIVERSITY OF MONTANA, MISSOULA, MONTANA 59801

Contents

Preface

If Ecclesiastical History is lifted beyond the parochial study of the Christian group in the western world and placed in the context of world religions, and the word *ekklesia* is understood to mean the assembly of people called out and made separate by their religion, we can see the importance of examining the history of the first century of a religious or ideological minority in a certain environment and trying to formulate paradigms of the life, growth, and death of each species. Thus a Marxist would be well advised to ruminate long over the History of early Christianity in the Mediterranean world; a Protestant Christian to consider deeply the real differences between Mahayana and Theravada Buddhism in so far as these can be discerned in the primal times.

Ugandan Islam is one of the miracles of modern Africa. Besides increasing rapidly in quality and numbers, it is active and progressive. It is an example, unique in its own way, of a religion from abroad that has been taken up, speedily assimilated and spread by African people whose own traditional structures had not broken down, who were far from the nearest great Islamic centers and who had little outside help or encouragement. In their early days they nearly took over the central Kingdom, Buganda, but were forestalled by the Christians. Under the British colonial regime they felt they were second-class citizens. At Independence time the emerging politicians found them an influential group and in General Amin they may have found their Constantine. Muslims are about ten percent of the present population of the country as a whole, but they exercise an influence out of proportion to mere numbers. Their distribution throughout the country is not even. In the northeast and southwest they are few, in the central regions and in the northwest they are a sizable proportion of the population. The reasons for this strong presence in some places and lack of penetration in others, as well as details of the interaction of Islam with the Traditional Religions and Christianity, have to be sought out through small-scale studies in the areas themselves. During the 1950s students at Makerere University College at Kampala who had the necessary equipment in language, background, and approach were encouraged by F. B. Welbourn to collect and bring in material on the religion of their own tribes or clans or religions. From 1963 onwards the Department of Religious Studies at Makerere held a regular seminar on "Religion in Contemporary Africa" where students and faculty reported back with tapes, documents, and artifacts on fieldwork. It was possible to submit results to joint study by the group in conjunction with the findings and presentations of others. Thus a student who had discovered in talking to old men that Muslim merchants a century ago had followed a certain route could be given corroboration by a more library-minded student whose task had been to follow the same point in printed material. This could include accounts by early European explorers, monograph studies, or periodicals like the *Uganda Journal.*

In 1967 with the help of a grant from the University of East Africa Committee which was seeking to encourage the production of textbooks based on local experience and research, it was possible to send out a mimeographed first report on our findings to schools and colleges, asking for criticism and offers of research material to fill lacunae. The information received in response was compiled in mimeographed form and in 1968 a revised report was sent out, for further criticism, use, and checking. Parts of it were "tried out" as lectures in 1969 at the African Studies Centers at Edinburgh and Aberdeen in Scotland and at the Boston meeting of the American Academy of Religion.

Since much of our material is based on historical documents, in the case of African words we have followed the old orthography with a few inconsistencies. With regard to terms of Indian or Arabic background we have kept to standard East African practice in the late colonial period but in a number of cases have at the first occurrence of the word given the modern scholarly transliteration. As to the time span to be covered, we have partly changed our minds as we have gone along. We agreed to stop at 1962, with the end of the colonial period; then we thought we might glance forward to the setting up of the National Association for the Advancement of Muslims in 1965 and the abolition of the Kingdoms in 1966-67. This work was completed by the end of 1970 but when early in 1971 a change of government took place in Uganda, it was difficult not to refer to that event, which in some ways rounds out our story.

We would have liked more time to collect further material and to present it less roughly, but unfortunately all three writers are at present away from the field and from specialist libraries. Arye Oded, a graduate of the Hebrew University who lived and studied in Uganda from 1962 to 1968, is now in Jerusalem; Abdu Kasozi, who is a Ugandan, having completed his first degree and teacher-qualification at Makerere University College, is taking a doctorate at the University of California, Santa Cruz; and Noel King, an Anglo-Indian who was Head of the Department of Religious Studies at Makerere University College from 1962 to 1968, is now on the faculty at Santa Cruz. It is therefore an interim report, 'a "semi-periodical" contribution to a rapidly ongoing corpus of study. It succeeds more in pointing to work that has not been done than to what has been done. It may even point to some that ought not to have been done. It is hoped that instead of adding anything to the already towering over-arching works on Islam in Africa, there is something here of the "nitty-gritty" of banana roots.

It is salutary to reflect on how expensive it is to put this kind of research before the public and a pleasure to acknowledge generous patrons. We thank the Makerere University College Research Committee, the Theological Education Fund of the World Council of Churches and the Rockefeller Foundation for the grants which made the field work possible; the Makerere University College and the University of East Africa Publications Committee and the Ford Foundation for a grant which paid for the first two compilations; the Research Committee of the University of California, Santa Cruz, whose help made it possible to transcribe, translate, and fill out a good deal of the material; and the American

Academy of Religion which subsidizes this Monograph Series. The libraries and stenographic services of these universities have also assisted greatly.

Many people have helped us. Our debts to Sheikh Hadad of Nakasero Mosque, Hakim Lukhman of Wandegeya, Sheikh Ahmed Nsambu of Natete, Sheikh Shuaib Ssemakula of Kawempe and Sheikh Ali Kalumba for tuition, companionship, love, and guidance are great. Dr. John Rowe of Northwestern, F. B. Welbourn of Bristol (England), and Said Hamdun of the University of Nairobi advised at the beginning, contributed material, and corrected drafts. Direct use of material submitted by Right Reverend Cyprian Bamwoze, Reverend Jerome Bamunoba, Mr. A. R. Dunbar, and Dr. Michael Twaddle is acknowledged as it is used. Those who have helped with advice, criticism, "leg-work," searching newspapers, translating, typing, and doing our work to free us to do this include Abdul Adatia, Rohit Barot, Philip Bell, Dorothy Bergen, Samuel Busulwa, Alan and Clare Claydon, Muhammad el Dessuky, Aziz Esmail, Joan Hodgson, Eric Hutchison, Yasmin Kanji, Francis, Naomi and Jeremy King, Matthias Kiwanuka, Robin Lamburn, Susan Liddicoat, Aloysius Lugira, Martin Mbwana, John Mbiti, William Mukasa, Amin Mutyaba, Azim Nanji, John Nsubuga, M. Louise Pirouet, Anne Reid, James Ritchie, Franz Schildknecht, S. von Sicard, and Patrick Vaughan. The writers also thank the Editor of the Monograph Series of the American Academy of Religion (Dr. Stephen D. Crites) for his patience, humor and encouragement, and the printers for their help and considerateness.

This was the last complete monograph on which Evelyn King worked as sub-editor, correcter of English, looker out of references, encourager, and typist of the first two drafts. (She also worked on chapters of two other books.) In the weeks before her death she remarked that if this were ever published it would be like the case reported in the newspapers of a baby born alive though its mother was on the pill and had had an abortion. This book has indeed been an unconscionable time atravailing. It has been rewritten at least twice over a four year period after a gestation of four years before that. It is not yet complete and inevitably shows the effects of changes of policy and persons. Responsibility for mistakes, expressions of tendentious opinions and invidious implications rests with Noel King who edited and compiled the whole. It is hoped, however, that this monograph contains otherwise inaccessible material which will be of use to scholars and those who follow it up. It is dedicated to the colloquy in learning we so richly enjoyed during the period of our study in Uganda with African Traditionalists, Christians, Hindus, Jews, and Muslims.

Oxford, Santa Cruz, and Jerusalem
Passover and Good Friday, 1972

Noel King
Abdu Kasozi
Arye Oded

ix

CHAPTER I

Islam in Pre-Colonial Buganda

1. THE COMING OF ISLAM TO BUGANDA

In telling of the rise and spread of Islam and its meeting with other
religions in Uganda, it is necessary to begin the story in the old central Kingdom
of Buganda, and then pass on to other parts of the country.[1] Oral traditions and
written sources agree that Islam was first brought from the south to Buganda in
the reign of Kabaka Suna (c. 1832-1856). The carriers of the new religion were
"Arabs" and "Waswahili." The former were men with some claim to descent
from Arabs who had come from southeast Arabia and the Persian Gulf region.
Since the decline of Portuguese power in the eighteenth century, the Sultans of
Muscat and Oman had maintained a claim to suzerainty over some of the
off-shore islands and the coastal towns of East Africa. In 1840 Seyyid Said made
Zanzibar his capital. Indian financiers and men of commerce were encouraged to
join in, and trade into inland Africa was promoted. The leaders in this opening
up of the continent were newly arrived Arabs as well as members of families

---

1   The root is -ganda; the place is Bu-ganda; the people, Ba-ganda (singular
    Mu-ganda); the language Lu-ganda. The country as a whole was given the name
    Uganda by the Europeans who employed the word the Swahili used for the old
    Kingdom of Buganda. For general background on Uganda see A Study Guide for
    Uganda by Terence K. Hopkins with the assistance of Perezi Kamunanwire
    (mimeo. African Studies Center, Boston University, 1969), and Angela Molnos,
    Die Sozialwissenschaftliche Erforschung Ostafrikas, 1954-1963 (Berlin,
    Heidelberg, New York, 1965). On the religions in this part of Africa see the
    bibliographies in Noel King's Religions of Africa (New York: Harper and Row,
    1970) and Christian and Muslim in Africa 1971). J. Spencer Trimmingham's
    Islam in East Africa (London and New York: Praeger, 1964), and The Influence
    of Islam upon Africa (London and New York: Oxford University Press, 1968),
    Joseph Schacht's "Notes on Islam in East Africa," Studia Islamica, 23 (1965) 91
    ff., as well as James Kritzeck and William H. Lewis, Islam in Africa (New York:
    Van Nostrand-Reinhold, 1969) give valuable material and bibliographies. For the
    history of Buganda and full bibliographic references see Semakula Kiwanuka's A
    History of Buganda (London: Longmans, 1971), a work of major importance in
    this field which unfortunately did not reach us till after this work was
    completed. Abdu K. Kasozi, The Spread of Islam in Uganda, which is to be
    published at Kampala, gives details of source material and statistics. For
    ethnographical background, including the Traditional Religions, the
    International African Institute's Ethnographical Surveys are indispensable and
    cover most of Uganda. Margaret Faller's The Eastern Lacustrine Bantu (London:
    International African Institute, 1960) is brilliant and a good place to start. For
    topographical details see The Uganda Atlas (Kampala: Government Printer,
    1962) and B. W. Langlands and A. Namirembe: Studies in the Geography of
    Religion in Uganda (Kampala: mimeographed, 1967).

which had been on the coast for some time and had intermarried with indigenous peoples.

In the meantime a much older meeting of Arab Muslim and African traditional cultures, which focuses in the Swahili language, had been going on in the area stretching from Lamu in the north to the Comoro Islands in the south. We are fortunate in possessing a constantly growing wealth of material about the religion and culture of the Swahili people who became the main early pioneers of Islam in Uganda.[2] Theirs was a form of Sunni Shafi [Arabic: shaf i] Islam, which had in some of its aspects, come to terms with African traditions. So far as one can generalize about a people and group it is commonly agreed that the Swahili are cheerful, easy-going, patient, and tolerant.

The Arabs and Swahili entered Buganda from the southeast. They crossed the Kagera River; then, if granted permission to proceed by the Kabaka, they went by way of Masaka and Kibibi in Butambala County to the capital which was located in the Kampala area.[3] Probably the first Muslim visitors to the region included Isa bin Husayn, a Baluch gunman who had served the Sultan of Zanzibar and had wandered into Uganda to get away from his creditors. He was generously received by Kabaka Suna and given land and a harem.[4] Snay ibn Amir from Oman was another early visitor. When Burton and Speke met him in 1857 in Tabora he had traveled into the interior a number of times and had visited Buganda in 1852. His agents had reached Busoga.[5] Another was Ahmed ibn Ibrahim al-Ameri who claimed to have visited Buganda in 1844.[6]

2   A. H. J. Prins: *The Swahili-Speaking Peoples of Zanzibar and the East African Coast* (London: International African Institute, 1961, rpt. 1967) remains the most accessible survey of the ethnography. On their religious law and customs see C. Velten, *Desturi Za Wasuaheli* (Goettingen, 1903, translated as *Sitten und Gebraeuche der Suaheli,* Goettingen, 1903). The autobiography of Tippu Tip (text and translation by W. H. Whiteley, Nairobi, 1966) gives a vivid picture of one of the greatest of the Swahili and Arab merchant adventurers.

3   Oral tradition collected along the route in January 1966 and checked in May 1967. J. H. Speke was in the area in 1862; see his *What Led to the Discovery of the Source of the Nile* (Edinburgh and London, 1863, rpt. 1908) and "The Upper Basin of the Nile," *Journal of the Royal Geographical Society,* 33 (1863). On the uses of oral material, see J. Vansina, *Oral Tradition* (London: Routledge and Kegan Paul, 1965) and M. S. M. Kiwanuka: "Reflections on the Role of Oral Traditions in the Writing of pre-colonial History in Africa," *Acta Africana,* 6, No. 1 (1967), 63-72.

4   R. F. Burton, *The Lake Regions of Central Africa* (1860; rpt. London and New York, 1961), II, 193. Burton was the most accomplished of the Victorian pornographers.

5   Burton, *The Lake Regions,* I, p. 324 f., Speke, *What Led to the Discovery,* p. 255.

6   See John Gray, "Ahmed ibn Ibrahim," *Uganda Journal,* 11 (1947), 80-97, and "Emin Diaries, Extract I," *Uganda Journal,* 25 (1961), 10. It is not

The efforts of the Muslim visitors to bring their religion to the Kabaka's attention may be seen in this description of an episode at Ganda court:

> Medi Ibulaimu rebuked Kabaka Suna for killing people every day saying: "There is Katonda [the creator god, hence god, or Allah] who created us, and you too, and he gives you this kingdom to rule your people." Suna replied: "I know there are many *balubaale* [spirits] who give me this kingdom." Ibulaimu went on preaching, but Suna paid no attention, till finally he [the Kabaka] said: "Who is this Katonda you go on talking about? Is he greater than I?" Ibulaimu said: "He is above and he will raise all whom he loves." Therefore Suna asked to "read" and read four chapters of the Qur'an before Ibulaimu left for good.[7]

It is not possible to be certain about which chapters these were because of the writer's distortion of the Arabic, but it is probable that the Kabaka learned at least to say the *bismillahi,* "in the name of God, the merciful the compassionate," the *fatiha,* "the Opener," and the last *surahs* of the Qur'an. Thus he would have learned of the oneness of God, his mercy, refuge in him from evil and malicious whisperers (witchcraft and sorcery), and his Lordship over jinns and men. Anyone who considers this incident is bound to admire the Muslim's courage. A traditional diviner who had rebuked the Kabaka had had his mouth sewn up and was not released till the Kabaka was awed by a lightning storm.[8]

The Kabaka treated the Muslim traders well. They were interested in ivory and slaves, and the Baganda traded with them for beads, firearms and eventually cloth. (Their own local cloth made from the hammered bark of the fig tree was clean and beautiful, while in the early days they considered cotton cloth to be smelly.) Towards the end of the reign of Suna there seems to have been a lull in trading or a breakdown of contact between the incoming traders and the court of Buganda. Islam had not had much opportunity to take root.

necessary for us at this point to go into the vexed question of this date, except to say it is probably too early. The last ten years of Suna's reign with a *terminus ante quem* in 1852 when Snay arrived are safe limits.

7   Apolo Kagwa, *Ebika Bya Baganda* (a title usually abbreviated to *Ebika*) (Kampala: Uganda Bookshop, 1906, rpt. 1949), 115f. The passage quoted was selected and translated by F.B. Welbourn. Louise Pirouet's *Dictionary of Christianity in Uganda,* (Makerere: mimeographed, 1969) is an invaluable guide to the biography of the great Uganda Christians. Kagwa had studied with the Muslims and served as Keeper of the King's mosque before he became a Christian in the 1880s. For an up−to−date and basic list of the Luganda writers see John Rowe, "Myth, Memoir and Moral Admonition, Luganda Historical Writing, 1839-1969," *Uganda Journal,* 33 (1969), 17−40, 217−219.

8   Apolo Kagwa, *Basekabaka be Buganda* (Kampala: Uganda Bookshop and Macmillan, editions in 1901, 1912, 1927; rpt. 1953), pp. 89 f.; hereafter abbreviated to *Basekabaka.*

2.   THE REIGN OF KABAKA MUTESA

Kabaka Suna's successor was Mutesa (c. 1856-1884), whose complicated and skillful manipulation of the forces amongst which his kingship was set makes him a competitor for being numbered among the top ten cleverest statesmen of the nineteenth century. One of the first Muslims to visit him was Ali Nakatukula who came in the late 1850s or early 1860s and had been among those who visited his father.[9] The King asked what his father had discussed with him and was told their conversation was about God and the rising from the dead. Mutesa asked to be taught "to read" - a technical term which includes not only reading as such but reading in the sense of "learning." Ali left his Swahili servant Makwega with Mutesa, and the King learnt quickly.

Muslim merchants, including Khamis ibn Abdullah who greatly influenced Mutesa, came from now on in a fairly steady stream. They read with the King themselves or left their servants to study with him. Luganda sources indicate that the King was an apt student, he learnt the alphabet and various chapters of the Qur'an and was able to render portions from Arabic into Luganda.[10]

Hamu Mukasa, who became a Christian later in the Kabaka's reign, has left a graphic description of Mutesa's progress in and enthusiasm for Islam in his early days:

> When Mutesa came to the throne, his father Suna had already tried this religion and had failed. So the Arabs tried to do all they could to teach Muhammad's religion to Kabaka Mutesa, because he was diligent in everything he was learning. That is why he was able to learn Muhammad's religion and to speak Swahili.
>
> Having learned Islam, he called his chiefs and told them how good this religion was; that there is only one God, called the Great, God the omnipotent, *Hakibalu,* who is greater than all the spirits. "I want you all to study this religion," he told them, and tried to teach them what he had learned, explaining to them the meaning of what he read from the Bible of the Muslims, called the Qur'an. His chiefs replied: "You, sir, have more wisdom

9   On Mutesa see M. S. M. Kiwanuka, *Mutesa of Uganda* (Kampala: East African Literature Board, 1967); D. A. Low, *Religion and Society in Buganda, 1875-1900,* East African Studies, No. 8 (Kampala, n.d.), is also most useful. Roland Oliver's *The Missionary Factor in East Africa* (London and New York: Longman, 1952) is classical and fundamental. On Ali see Kagwa, *Ebika,* 117.

10   Oral statement by Sheikh Ahmad Nsambu at Natete, 9 March 1967; Kagwa, *Basekabaka,* 123, *Ebika,* 117; J. T. K. Gomotoka, *Makula kye Kitabo kye Kika Ekilangira Ky'olulyo lwe Buganda,* MS, (abbreviated *Makula),* 6, 2496 f. This manuscript written in a neat copper-plate hand is a multi-volume work of which two are missing, and was written perhaps around 1924-1926. The author was head of the Prince's clan. The manuscript is in the care of P. B. Lukongwa, the present Sabalangira, who graciously allowed Arye Oded to put a photo-copy of volumes 3 and 6 in Makerere Library.

than we in understanding difficult things such as these. If you appreciate and accept them, so do we. Let us embrace the religion; since you are there to teach us to know all and to understand about God."

Then the Kabaka ordered all the people to pray regularly. Thereupon his chiefs said to him: "Learning this religion and loving its books after the example of Your Majesty will replace the hunting of animals, and your chiefs together with all your people will certainly learn to love this religion like you."

On hearing this the Kabaka became very pleased, and dogs used for hunting were henceforth disliked because of the religion which does not like them. Then Islam gained ground more and more, to the extent that failure to have the stone used for Muslim prayers in one's courtyard meant endangering one's life, because it would be disobedience to the royal command.

Orders were given out to be kept by all; whoever transgressed them would be convicted or could be put to death. These were the orders:
1. Everbody had to pray during the hours of prayer.
2. Everybody had to fast during the period of fasting.
3. No one was allowed to eat unlawful meat, that is, meat not killed by one recognized as a true Muslim.

Only circumcision was not obligatory, because the King himself was not circumcized. Everyone was free to be circumcized for the sake of his faith. Thus many came to be circumcized without being forced at all, and became members of Islam out of their own choice and not because of the Kabaka.

At this period the Kabaka sent out his messengers to inspect who were observing the religious laws and who were not. Among those messengers was one called Kakoloboto, sent to Buwaya, a part of Busiro county. This man happened to break the Kabaka's orders and was caught eating during the Fast. Consequently he was accused by those whom he used to arrest for breaking the Fast and from whom he used to take heavy bribes of cows, goats, and other things. He was convicted of breaking the orders of his King who sent him; there arose a proverb from him saying: "You are Kakoloboto who cheated the Fast while forcing others to observe it," meaning that you order others to do good while you are doing evil.

Then, because the Kabaka favored this religion so much and liked to please its adherents too, he made it a law that whoever did not read (did not belong to the religion) would not succeed his father and those who did not read should be arrested and put to death. A host of messengers were sent out everywhere in all the counties and they arrested a lot of people, perhaps two thousand and more, and killed them in many various and cruel ways - burning, spearing, and drowning them - on the grounds that they were pagans, they had refused to embrace the religion ordered by the King to all his subjects. The Kabaka and the leading men of the religion thought that this would oblige the rest of the people to embrace the religion. Many in fact who did not care for the religion before, terrified by the massacre of their fellow men, started learning it. They started putting stones in their courtyards, making boards on which they could learn to read, and making mats to pray on in order to be considered religious. All the while this was a means of saving their lives and not for any interest in the religion as such. Some perhaps liked this way of treating the people, hoping that it would help to spread the religion and to increase its strength in all the people. This, however, turned out not to be the case, because those upon whom it was forced did not embrace it in truth. [11]

11 *Simuda nyuma* (abbreviated *Simuda*) (London: S.P.C.K., 1938), passages

As we shall see later, Mutesa, in his enthusiasm, even sent a mission to the neighboring kingdom Bunyoro which was rejected by Kabarega. Hamu Mukasa continues:

> Kabaka Mutesa was very saddened on receiving this reply and said, "I am very sorry that that brother of mine has rejected the religion of God and has trusted in his own dignity and his gods alone. I regret that he thinks only in terms of this present life to which he compares the life to come. Let it be so, but I feel sorry for him to remain in the ancient customs of the *balubaale* whom we called gods while there is the true God, the Creator. You, my subjects, however, persevere in the religion." Unanimously all the chiefs replied: "We shall persevere thus; and since you are our leader, we will follow you wherever you go."

The King's keenness for Islam was shown in other ways as well. He built a mosque and appointed a caretaker and caller to prayer. He kept the daily and Friday prayers. The slaughtering of animals for meat was now to be carried out in the Muslim way by circumcized butchers. [12] (This is a monopoly claimed by Muslims in Uganda to this day). Mutesa observed Ramadan for the first time in 1867 and is said to have gone on doing so ten times. [13] Interminable exchanges of courteous salutations is typical of the beauty of Kiganda manners; Mutesa tried to substitute the (comparatively) briefer Muslim greetings. His acceptance of the Muslim doctrines of the resurrection may have been behind his interference with royal burial customs. Normally the jawbones of Kings were removed and buried separately. Mutesa tried to bring together bodies and jawbones for his predecessors and forbade such dissection for himself. [14]

Mutesa had refused circumcision - only with difficulty do Baganda overcome their abhorrence of this operation. The horror would be intensified when it concerned the person of a sacral king who had to be whole and perfect. The Ashanti still take the same view with regard to the Ashantihene. In any case, such an act might have given powerful traditionalists an excuse to depose Mutesa. He experimented by sending one of his pages to be circumcized and then gave permission for anyone to submit to it if he wished. Muslim jurisconsults in Uganda to this day debate whether Mutesa's uncircumcision made him a non-Muslim, and some (following at this point the Maliki school of

from pp. 14-17; translated by Dr. F. X. Mbazira. *Hakibalu* is presumably *al-akhbar,* and the stones in the compounds the stones on which they stood for ablutions.

12   Gomotoka, *Makula,* 6, 2506, 2497, 2498.

13   Kagwa, *Basekabaka,* 130, 124; Gomotoka, *Makula,* 6, 2499; Ali Kulumba, *Ebyafayo By'Obuisramu mu Uganda* (Katwe, Kampala), 1953, p. 3; hereafter abbreviated *Ebyafayo.*

14   Apolo Kagwa, *Empisa Za Baganda* (Kampala: Uganda Bookshop, 1952), 77 f., 14, *Basekabaka,* 125; Kalumba, *Ebyafayo,* 3.

law) say it is possible for a Muslim to take the view that it would have been desirable for him to follow *sunna* (custom) in being circumcized, but it is not an absolute obligation. Unfortunately for this view most Muslims in Uganda follow the Shafite school of law and not the Maliki. [Arabic: *Maliki*] Many of the learned Muslims in Uganda know their Bibles well and point out that Abraham was circumcized at the age of ninety.[15]

A number of unbelievers [*bakafiri*, may we call them "pagan martyrs"?] paid with their lives for their refusal to adopt Muslim practices at the command of the King.[16] Then the turn of the Muslims came, in the middle 1870s. A blood-thirsty persecution of Muslims which we shall shortly describe took place. Though the main reason for this *volte face* was probably the disobedience of the pages to the Kabaka's command, no doubt the threat from the north of Egyptian domination played a part in it, so it would be as well if we went back a few years before 1875 to outline the nature of this danger.

Muhammad Ali, an Albanian soldier sent by the Turks, had been the virtual ruler of Egypt since early in the century and had gradually exerted Egyptian influence up the Nile. By 1839 his officers had reached Gondokoro, a thousand miles south of Khartoum, but there a cataract had held things up. The Khedive Ismail (1863-1879) ordered Samuel Baker to push southwards, and in 1872 he built posts at Fatiko not far from Gulu in Acholi and at Masindi in Bunyoro (which are both in modern Uganda). Baker found that traders from the north, most of whom were Muslim by religion, had raided whole districts for slaves and ivory and loot and were hated and feared as far afield as Buganda.[17] Baker himself ran into difficulties with the young Omukama Kabarega of

15   Based on oral material collected at Natete (Sheikh Ahmad Nsambu, 9 March 1967) and Kawempe (Sheikh Shuaib Semakula, 12 March).

16   On the pagan martyrs, see Hamu Mukasa, *Simuda Nyuma*, p. 16; Kagwa, *Basekabaka*, p. 129; B. Musoke Zimbe, *Ebyafayo by'obwakabaka bwe Buganda, Buganda ne Kabaka* (Kampala, 1939), p. 25. There is a copy in Makerere Library with a translation of parts by F. Kamoga.

17   The main outline of events is based on Roland Oliver and Gervase Mathew, eds., *History of East Africa*, I (London & New York: Oxford University Press, 1963). See also Samuel Baker, *Ismailia*, II (London: Macmillan, 1874), 98, 117, 136 f.; M. F. Shukry, *Equatoria under Egyptian Rule* (Cairo: Cairo University Press, 1953) gives a fascinating selection of letters. E. Linant de Bellefonds, "Itineraire (fev. - juin 1875)." *Bulletin trimestriel de la societe Khedival de geographie du Caire, ser.* 1 (1876-1877), 1-104, makes enthralling reading but is difficult of access. Samuel Baker (1821-1893) was a Londoner who used his inheritance to finance travels and exploration in Ceylon, the Middle East, Europe, and Africa. His successor, Charles George Gordon (1833-1885) was a British officer who had served in the Crimea and China (where ironically enough, since he was a devoted Christian, he put down the only Christian mass-movement China has known) before entering the Khedive's service. He was killed in the first Sudanese Independence Movement.

Bunyoro and beat a retreat. It seems reasonable to suppose that the bad behavior of men like these connected with Egypt, which was considered to be a Muslim power, damaged the cause both of Islam and Egypt.

In 1874 Gordon took over responsibility for the Egyptian thrust to the south. Kabaka Mutesa requested a Muslim teacher and other help from him. Gordon sent various expeditions to Buganda and Mutesa managed to frustrate all "their politics and their knavish tricks." He demoralized the commander of one expedition by graciously presenting a woman to each of his soldiers. Thinking Gordon, as a servant of Egypt, must be a Muslim, Mutesa emphasized his own Islam: learning Gordon was a Christian, he leaned in that direction. In January 1876 Gordon sent Nur Aga with some troops and a Muslim teacher to Mutesa. The soldiers behaved atrociously, and Mutesa considered that the Egyptians had despised his kind of Islam.

Hamu Mukasa says that in 1873 (his dates are not always so accurate as to forbid a leeway of a year or two) a group of "Turks" visited the Kabaka and criticized the orientation of his mosque, and his carelessness in allowing uncircumcized men to slaughter animals and lead the prayers and the community. These criticisms led to fear on the part of the old men lest they be forced into a stricter Islam and to insubordination on the part of some young men who preferred the full following of Allah's precepts to the Kabaka's form of Islam. Mutesa owed his position to a balance of the powers about him and clearly Islam had reached a point of strength where a decision about it would have to be made.[18]

In the meantime Henry Morton Stanley visited Mutesa (April 1875) and found him so open to the possibilities of a Christian mission that he sent off his famous letter which appeared in the *Daily Telegraph* on 15 November 1875. It deserves study in some detail, for by June 1877 it had brought in the missionaries, and it brilliantly illustrates the thought of Stanley and his Victorian contemporaries:[19]

18   This account is based on Hamu Mukasa, *Simuda Nyuma*, 18-29. The detailed discussion of events and dates should be followed in Ahmed Katumba and F. B. Welbourn, "Muslim Martyrs of Buganda," *Uganda Journal,* 28, 2, (1964), 151-163.

19   H. M. Stanley, *Through the Dark Continent*, (London: George Newness, 1899 edition), volume I, 164. The source material provided by the Christian missions is varied in nature and overwhelming in volume. For instance, the Church Missionary Society's activities can be followed in *A. M. Mackay by his Sister*, London, 1890; R. P. Ashe: *Two Kings of Uganda* (London: Sampson, Low, 1889) and *Chronicles of Uganda*, London, 1894; in the writings of Roscoe, their missionary anthropologist; their local archives now at Makerere; their London archives and in their periodicals, *Ebifa Mu Buganda, Mengo Notes,* the *Gleaner* and *Intelligencer*. The White Fathers' material may be sought at Via Aurelia in Rome, locally, and in *Munno,* a brilliant Luganda Newspaper - details are given in J. F. Faupel: *African Holocaust* (London: Chapman, 1962). See also the full bibliography given by H. P. Gale: *Uganda and the Mill Hill Fathers*

I have, indeed, undermined Islamism so much here that Mtesa has determined henceforth, until he is better informed, to observe the Christian Sabbath as well as the Muslim Sabbath, and the great captains have unanimously consented to this. He has further caused the Ten Commandments of Moses to be written on a board for his daily perusal - for Mtesa can read Arabic - as well as the Lord's Prayer and the golden commandment of our Savior, "Thou shalt love thy neighbor as thyself." This is great progress for the few days that I have remained with him, and, though I am no missionary, I shall begin to think that I might become one if such success is feasible. But oh! that some pious, practical missionary would come here! What a field and harvest ripe for the sickle of civilization! Mtesa would give him anything he desired - houses, lands, cattle, ivory, etc.! He might call a province his own in one day. It is not the mere preacher, however, that is wanted here. The bishops of Great Britain collected, with all the classic youth of Oxford and Cambridge, would effect nothing by mere talk with the intelligent people of Uganda. It is the practical Christian tutor, who can teach people how to become Christians, cure their diseases, construct dwellings, understand and exemplify agriculture, and turn his hand to anything, like a sailor - this is the man who is wanted. Such a one, if he can be found, would become the saviour of Africa. He must be tied to no church or sect, but profess God and His Son and the moral law, and live a blameless Christian, inspired by liberal principles, charity to all men, and devout faith in Heaven. He must belong to no nation in particular but to the entire white race. Such a man or men, Mtesa, Emperor of Uganda, Usogo, Unyoro, and Karagwe - an empire 360 geographical miles in length, by 50 in breadth - invites to repair to him. He has begged me to tell the white men that, if they will only come to him, he will give them all they want. Now, where is there in all the pagan world a more promising field for a mission than Uganda? Colonel Linant de Bellefonds is my witness that I speak the truth, and I know he will corroborate all I say. The Colonel, though a Frenchman, is a Calvinist, and has become as ardent a wellwisher for the Waganda as I am. Then why further spend needlessly vast sums upon black pagans of Africa who have no example of their own people becoming Christians before them? I speak to the Universities Mission at Zanzibar and to the Free Methodists at Mombasa, to the leading philanthropists, and the pious people of England. "Here, gentlemen, is your opportunity - embrace it! The people on the shores of the Nyanza call upon you. Obey your own generous instincts, and listen to them; and I assure you that in one year you will have more converts to Christianity than all other missionaries united can number. The population of Mtesa's kingdom is very dense; I estimate the number of his subjects at 2,000,000. You need not fear to spend money upon such a mission, as Mtesa is sole ruler, and will repay its cost tenfold with ivory, coffee, otter skins of a very fine quality, or even in cattle, for the wealth of this country in all these products is immense. The road here is by the Nile, or via Zanzibar, Ugogo, and Unyanyembe. The former route, so long as Colonel Gordon governs the countries of the Upper Nile, seems the most feasible."

At some time before the arrival of the missionaries the Muslim Martyrdoms occurred.[20] The Kabaka appears to have grown increasingly

(London, 1959). Most unfortunately we were not able to work on the Verona Fathers' material at Gulu and in Italy which is so important for northern and western Uganda, though cordially invited to do so.

20   See Katumba and Welbourn, "Muslim Martyrs of Buganda," *Uganda*

annoyed by the refusal of his islamically inclined pages to obey his orders and their insolence in despising his form of religion. He ordered that they be tortured and killed. Some were burned, some drowned, some left to die of exposure and pain after their arms and legs had been broken. The Luganda sources bear witness to the courage of the young Muslims who preferred to obey God rather than the Kabaka. Muslim scholars of the present day in Buganda connect the Kabaka's decision to turn against Islam with the Egyptian threat and the coming of Stanley. The explorer with his rough manliness, showmanship and military prowess apparently took advantage of Mutesa's wavering to present the possibility of Christianity. He was certainly a strange apostle. On the other hand, a careful reading of the older writers, such as Kagwa and Hamu Mukasa, indicates that the cause of the persecution was more on the side of the Traditional Religion: the young Muslims found the Kabaka too slow in moving into proper Islam, the traditionalists took the chance to repress them with force.

Facts do not warrant the supposition that Islam remained under a cloud for long. There is little evidence of any further steps being taken against Islam between 1877 and Mutesa's death in 1884. In June 1880 the Kabaka proclaimed Islam's special position in the country, and in 1881 he revived his own allegiance to that religion. Powerful Muslim influences remained at court and the work of Islam continued in the countryside. The Kabaka flirted with Christianity. He

showed great interest but was not baptized; he played off Protestants against Catholics, Christians against Muslims. In the background the traditionalists remained powerful, and it was not beyond the realm of the possible that the Kabaka should declare himself one of them and try to chase the new religions out.

3.   THE WARS OF RELIGION

Kabaka Mutesa died in 1884 and his successor, Mwanga, had to face a triangle of innovating forces - Catholic (nicknamed Bafalansa since the White Fathers were mainly French and the Baganda tend to change "r" to "l"), Protestant (labeled Bangereza since the Church Missionary Society appeared to be mainly English, *pace* her many Irish and Scots), and Muslim (Basiramu) - quite apart from the increasing desire of the reactionaries to keep things in the old ways. In late 1885 and during 1886 and 1887 he carried out a persecution of Christians.[21] Then he tried to eliminate Christians and Muslims together. They united to fight him and then turned on one another. In the wars the Muslims made an excellent showing. They were well led and had some firearms and

Journal, 28, (1964) 151-163, and T. W. Gee, "A Century of Muhammadan Influence in Buganda, 1852-1951," *Uganda Journnal,* 22 (1958), 139-150.

21   These were the martyrs honored by the Pope's visit to Uganda in 1969. Faupel, *African Holocaust,* and J. V. Taylor, *The Growth of the Church in Buganda* (London: S.C.M. Press, 1958) are good places to start a detailed study.

powder supplied to them by the Arabs and Swahili. In 1967 it was still possible to visit veterans of these battles. Here is the substance of one recording.[22] Osmani Wamala said:

I was circumcized after the death of Mutesa at a time when people were joining Muslims secretly and individually: they used to meet in the banana groves. Natete, where the Kabaka had first placed the Muslim visitors on their arrival, was still a center of Muslim influence. The Baganda chose and copied the religion of the Arabs, it was at their own asking, for the Arabs were traders, not preachers. Many Baganda, on becoming Muslim, became traders, and they started preaching.

The Kabaka decided to maroon the Christians and Muslims on an island in Lake Nalubaale. We suspected a trap and revolted. The Muslims moved up to Rubaga and attacked Mengo, while the Catholics attacked from the Kampala side. We, the readers, were now coming out in the open at long last and the men of religion were dethroning the King. On driving him out we installed little Kiwewa.

The men of the three religions were all working together. They met to divide up the offices, the Katikiro was a Catholic: the Mukwenda, a Protestant; and the Pokino, the Omujasi and the Kawuta, Muslims.[23] Then some Catholics refused this settlement, and the Muslims joined those without religion[24] to fight against the Bafalansa and Bangereza, who were chased away. The Kabaka (Mutebi II, called Kiwewa) summoned us and our leaders went. Kapalaga was mutilated as to his genitals and then shot with a gun. Some of our leading men were killed. We heard firing and took it that our leaders had been killed so we assaulted the royal enclosure, drove away Kiwewa, and being now in control, looked for someone to make Kabaka.

22   Interviews with Osmani Wamala at Buyenga, Butambala County, May and
     September 1967. Guide: Amin Mutyaba; interlocutors, Abdu Kasozi, Noel
King, William Montgomery Watt; *ad hoc* translation from the tape by J. E.
Nsubuga, revised in the Department of Religious Studies, Makerere. It is
remarkable how closely this oral account corresponds with Bakale Mukasa bin
Mayanja, *Akatabo ke Byafayo Eby'entalo za Kabaka Mwanga, Kiwewa ne
Kalema,* [The Book of the *Wars of Kings Mwanga, Kiwewe and Kalema]*
(Kyanjinja, Bulemezi, 1932; Katwe Press: Kampala, 1937 and 1954). Compare
also Abdul Karim Nyanzi,, *Ntalo Ze Dini mu Buganda,* [The Wars of Religion in
Buganda] (Katwe Press, Kampala, n.d.) and Abudala Sekimwanyi, *Ebyafayo
Ebitonotono Kudini Ye Kiyisiramu Okuyingira mu Buganda,* [A Short History
of the Coming of Islam to Buganda (Katwe Press: Kampala, 1947). The original
tape is in Makerere Library. The material given is a direct quotation without the
pauses and digressions of the spoken word. A version translated directly from a
copy of the tape has been published in King, *Christian and Muslim in Africa.*

23   Prime Minister and ministers in charge of Ssingo, of Buddu, warfare, and
     the Royal Kitchen respectively.

24   The word for religion is *dini* from the Arabic and Swahili and normally
     applies to Islam and Christianity. The followers of the African Traditional
Religion could be known as "men without religion," see Welbourn, *Makerere
Journal,* 4 (1960), 37. Muslim sources sometimes call such a man *kafir,* and the
Christian also use some form of *paganus.*

Kiwewa was not circumcized; time had been short and really he was against the Muslims. In the morning we made Kalema Kabaka, we drove away the Bafalansa and Bangereza. We remained in full and open control for two years.[25]

The Christians gathered strength and attacked us. Though we won a number of battles, we had to fall back. While we were being driven along, Kiwewa, who was a prisoner, was killed and about ten princes and fifty princesses got burnt in a fire while they were prisoners.[26]

After our defeat the Arabs locked themselves up following the example of Mackay and Mapera earlier on, and these Europeans were in the end allowed free passage to their friends by the Muslims.[27] But our enemies massacred the Arabs, they were burnt at their rest house at Natete, though they were guests in the country. Lugard rebuked them, but it was too late.

Kalema, after fleeing to various places, set up his capital at Kijungute.[28] It was there our Kabaka died. We made Mbogo, son of Suna, our leader. The Christians were still attacking and pushed us towards Bunyoro. A year or two later, Lugard sent messengers to say he wanted Mbogo to eat Buganda and then came to meet him with Nubians from Toro. He sat close like you are seated and said: "Bwana Mbogo, you should not let yourself and all these perish with you; there should not be all this bloodshed. My purpose is to reconcile you." Mbogo gave his agreement and the European asked if we also concurred. He questioned us as to whether we wanted villages given to us and we all assented. He granted us this country (Butambala) and we surrendered our weapons.

The old warrior's account recaptures the breathless adventure of those days but telescopes events in places. In 1890 Kabaka Mwanga was restored and

25   Kalema, son of Mutesa, is the *beau ideal* of Ugandan Islam - tall, light-colored, generous, brave. His posthumous son was Ramazane Ndawula. Welbourn in a letter states: "the dates are 10 September 1888 Kiwewa, 22 October 1888 Kalema, 11 October 1889 Mwanga, 26 November 1889 Kalema (again), 12 February 1890 Mwanga. See Sir John Gray: 'The Year of the Three Kings of Buganda,' *Uganda Journal,* 14 (1950), 23-49. Lugard did not arrive till December 1890." It is clear that the old man's account is difficult to reconcile with the accepted dating but he is recalling the sweep of events many years later. For Lugard's own account of the events see Margery Perham, ed., *The Diaries of Lord Lugard* (London and Evanston, Ill., 1959), II, 125-171; III, 240-268.

26   Prince Mbogo, son of Suna and brother of Mutesa who later became leader of the Muslims, was born probably in 1835 and survived this massacre as he had the customary killing of the princes and princesses at the beginning of the reign when Mwanga succeeded.

27   Mackay was a layman of the C. M. S.; *Mapera* was the Luganda name for the White Father, Lourdel (*mon père*). Although the old gentleman brought this incident in at this point, it is probable that his memory has blurred events or it is an aside.

28   Kijungute has become a kind of holy place to the Baganda Muslims. A *duwa* book written there was exhibited at the Uganda Museum in 1960. To this day men will boast that their father was a man of Kijungute.·

Lord Lugard arrived at the end of the year. A civil war broke out between Catholics and Protestants and it may have been during this that Lugard thought of a Muslim Kabaka. If he made such a promise, he did little to implement it. In 1893 the Muslims again rose in arms as a result of misunderstanding and mishandling and although Prince Mbogo held aloof he was deported to Zanzibar for three years. He profited by his visit to a Muslim country. In 1897 he returned home and carefully avoided being involved in the uprising of Nubian troops. They were Muslim to a man and had just grievances, but once the British brought up Indian troops and other help, the Nubi had little hope of success.

Under the colonial regime the Prince kept his own court and household. In the agreement of 1900 he and his followers were given twenty-four square miles of land, but he never seems to have gotten it demarcated. His Katikiro (Prime Minister, Chief Executive Officer), Taibu Magato, was a strong man who became a legend. Despite horrifying roads in the area, his tomb is still visited with awe.

The Muslims did not retain the position apparently promised them by Lugard, and year after year they complained of unfairness in the distribution of chieftainships. Butambala remains in many ways a Muslim country and traveling there from Lukalu to Kibibi and Kabasanda is reminiscent of *dar-al-Islam*. Like some Christians and Jews, some strict Muslims believe in the need of the equivalent of a Christendom or Zion or Pakistan, a place that is theirs, where they can really be themselves. Luckily for the propagation of Islam, Muslims are much wider spread than any one area and are able, as a result, to represent their religion the better and influence the nation as a whole.

At this point topographically and chronologically it would make good sense to describe the coming and spread of Islam in Uganda outside Buganda, but it is better to leave that till after something has been said of the fortunes of Islam during the colonial period, again using Buganda as our center because source material is at its most abundant there and because conditions in Buganda at that time closely affected the rest of the country so that in some matters something said of Buganda in colonial times was largely true of Uganda as a whole.

CHAPTER II

The Colonial Heyday

1. ISLAM'S CONTINUED PROGRESS

Already African historians recognize the colonial period as but a short episode in their long history.[1] In the late sixties a visitor could still talk to old people who had seen Lord Lugard and his Maxim gun. But for those who imposed colonial rule and those who underwent it, its years were interminable. To them too it looked as if the Muslims had played the power game and had lost: the Christians had all the advantages. The royal family and the ruling class had nearly been brought to Islam but now only one significant member of the royal house, Prince Nuhu Mbogo, was Muslim. In chieftainships, with all their patronage, Muslims were grossly outnumbered. The British rulers exercising overrule, that is, over that of the chiefs, were supposed to give fair play to Muslims. This was the declared policy of the Empire, and many British officers had a genuine admiration for the manly and military qualities Islam imbued. Even so the British administrators were themselves of Christian background even if they were not personally believers. In Uganda at the beginning of colonial rule they were suspicious of the Muslims because of their demonstrated ability to organize a fighting force and oppose the imperial power. Thus, though the colonial power was not supposed to interfere with religion, there is justification for the allegation that the British in Uganda in their early days favored Christianity (especially in its Anglican form) and dealt Islam some deft underhand blows.

Not many hours of study in the Uganda Government Archives at Entebbe can produce a gem of unfair dealing like the following. Harry Johnston who was Special Commissioner in Uganda from 1899 to 1901 was informed that Saleh, a chief in Busoga, was using his position to spread Islam. Johnston, who was not conspicuous for exhibiting either Christian faith or practice, wrote to the sub-commissioner of that area:

1   From the time of the establishment of colonial rule the number of relevant
     books, periodicals, newspapers, and pamphlets become so many that it is
     beyond the scope of this essay to mention even a fraction of them. The second
     and third volumes of the *Oxford History of East Africa* give a reliable
     conspectus. Improtant unpublished government archival material was consulted
     at the Public Records Office in London and at the Government archives at
     Entebbe. It is probable that some relevant and untapped material perished in the
     fire at the *lubiri* (royal enclosure) in May 1966. Reliable oral tradition for most
     of the period is still available in Uganda and is being systematically recorded by
     the Makerere Departments of Religious Studies and of History.

It is not in the interests of the British government that Mohammedanism should receive any more adherents than we can help in Uganda as Muslims are proverbially difficult to manage and are always in their hearts opposed to the administration of a Christian power. In Uganda itself we are obliged to put up with the existence of people of this faith because they were here before we came; but I can see that it is decidedly not to the interests of the British government that we should actually assist the spread of this religion - if you are convinced that a religious propaganda of this kind is being carried on by Saleh, arrest him and send him to Entebbe [the colonial government center]. It is particularly necessary at the present time that we should have no Mohammedan nonsense.[2]

The Muslims had come bringing an exciting new world and an advanced education and technology, but the Christians could command world resources and provide the latest "know-how" (a word beloved by Ugandans in the 1960s). "In colonial days the Muslims could not reach out to friends abroad; Egypt and Algeria were under the colonialists, Pakistan did not yet exist, Turkey was to be dismembered. The Christians could call in men and money from Europe and America to build· schools for them, to curry favor with their fellow whitemen [sic] in the government, to teach them science and provide instruction in modern devices. To whom could the Muslims turn? They were condemned to be a nation of butchers and heavy lorry drivers."[3]

At the same time the Muslims were divided among themselves. Up till his death in 1921 Prince Mbogo held the community together, but then there was a difference of opinion about his successor. His son, Prince Badru, was young, and, as is usual in Islam, people were not lacking to point out that leadership·is not necessarily in a family but should go to the most learned and pious. It was also pointed out that religious leadership did not necessarily follow political. This dispute became inextricably involved with an altercation over the Friday (Juma) Prayer. Sheikh Haji Sekimwanyi,. who was one of the first Ugandans to go on pilgrimage and return, urged people to pray the Friday prayer by itself at the

2   Johnston to sub-commissioner in Busoga, 3 December 1900, Entebbe Archives, Busoga Outward, A 11/1/53. On the writer, see Roland Oliver, *Sir Harry Johnston and the Scramble for Africa* (London: Chatto and Windus, 1957).

3   Abubakr Mayanja in a speech to the Makerere Muslim Brotherhood, *Id al-Fitr*, 1964. This gentleman has been called the Ugandan Disraeli. In 1952 he was sent down from Makerere for leading a food strike; he went on to Cambridge and London and returned to practise as a lawyer. He went into politics and suffered imprisonment under President Obote. He has served Buganda and Uganda as Minister of Education. He has access to Muslim archival material in the household of Prince Badru which may go back to Nuhu Mbogo's day. It is hoped that when he gets leisure he will write a history of Islam in Uganda. The Makerere Muslim Brotherhood has published over the years since 1958 a mimeographed *Journal* which is full of articles by Muslim students who have risen high in the East African world. Unfortunately, a complete set of this is not available. Welbourn notes that Muslims also monopolize the taxi service.

great congregational meetings on Fridays as Muslims did abroad at major centers. The others, who had Prince Badru assisted by Sheikhs Khalfan bin Mubaraka and Shuaib Ssemakula as their leaders, said both the Friday as well as the normal daily noon prayers (called *Zukuli* in Luganda). This was local practice going back to the early days of Islam's first coming to Uganda. The struggle was protracted and tedious with the colonial and Bugandan governments trying to get acceptable mediation and failing. It has been possible to obtain access to the complete dossier of papers of one of the groups which shows that disputes over land were as important as religion and personalities in the struggle.[4] In 1948 after Sheikh Sekimwanyi was dead, Sheikh Ahmadu Nsambu as leader of the Natete-Bukoto-Juma group made overtures to the Prince with the good offices of Sheikh Shuaib, and an agreement was reached. A certain number of splinter groups remained, but the main schism had been repaired.

Despite these apparently insuperable disadvantages Islam went from strength to strength during the colonial period. In the first place the colonialists, especially the soldiers, had a great admiration for a religion which has many affinities with British public (i.e. private) school religion. We even hear of a District Commissioner becoming a Muslim and greatly assisting his new religion. Many others detested Christian missions for making Africans "uppish." At the very least they feared Muslim public opinion in India, Egypt, and Iraq too much to infringe the British policy laid down by Queen Victoria not to interfere with religion.

It is possible to argue that, given the colonial situation, Islam, far from being at a disadvantage, had some wonderful opportunities which she did not fail to use, and moreover she avoided the taint of being directly associated with the ugly features of colonialism. Thus the British and Indians built a railroad from the east coast to Uganda which enabled Muslims from the Persian Gulf, Arabia, and the Swahili coast to come in and Ugandan Muslims to use the ocean steamer services from Mombasa to go to Arabia and Iraq. The German lake-steamer, road, and rail route across Tanganyika helped in the same way. The British set up a river-steamer, road, and rail service which brought Egyptians and Sudanese visitors and enabled Ugandans to travel to Khartoum and Cairo or to go across to Port Sudan to take ship across the Red Sea to Jeddah and thence to Mecca.

It is not easy to assess the volume and effect of this opening up of international travel for Muslims in East Africa. Apparently two Ugandans of Indian background went to Mecca in 1910. It is not till 1920 that we learn of two

4   Traditional Muslims do not think in terms of the modern European concept of a separation between sacred and secular. Some of these papers of the Natete-Bukoto Juma group have been photocopied with permission and deposited in Makerere Library. A careful writing up with citation of official documents by Sheikh Ahmed Nsambu of Natete has also been deposited. This Sheikh also gave staff and students generously of his time in many an interview. F. B. Welbourn points out that the name "Shuaib" is difficult in Luganda because of the absence of "h" in that language. The Sheikh spells his name as given, Baganda usually pronounce it "Swaibu."

Baganda going on the *hajj* (the Pilgrimage to Mecca). Haji Bakale died there but Abdalla Ssekimwaniji got home safely.[5] Increasingly larger numbers were going on the pilgrimage after World War II. They brought back Zam-Zam water with wonderful powers of healing, an indelible impression of the strength and brotherhood of Islam and the latest ideas on Muslim custom, fashion, devotion, and the calendar. The gathering to send off the pilgrims has become a national social event and jet-charter flights yearly make it possible for more and more people to go.

Not only did colonial rule open up international travel, roads, and steam-boat services, but within each colonial territory the model T Ford penetrated into formerly closed areas. Every corner of the country was penetrated, centers of trade and administration sprang up. Muslims went to these places as traders and minor officials - interpreters, storekeepers, watchmen, police. Often the British District Officer took with him a cook, an interpreter, a clerk, and some constables. Most of these were recruited among the Muslims. Unlike his Muslim servants he had little direct contact with the local people. They could respectably and legally take a wife locally, their children were Muslims, they lived among the people and at the same time were enviable and powerful.

While traditional society was intact, no new religion could go deep unless it converted the ruling class. Christianity did this in Buganda and, as we shall see, in Ankole and Bunyoro. But as a cash economy, modern government and better communications came in, the old societies began to break up. People reached out towards the new religions. In a mission school or parish church community they came into touch with Christianity. They met Islam by the wayside, in the market, in the village, while traveling, while enduring the law's delays, or waiting for the ferry.[6]

Islam had no missions comparable with those of the Christians - the Ahmaddiyya mission, which we shall mention later, did not arrive till late in the colonial period and did not, in Uganda, deploy resources equivalent to even a small Christian mission. But every Muslim was in another sense a missionary, he

5   The two men who went in 1910 were Khimji and Sulemohammed Bhanji.
     Regarding the *hajj* in Uganda acting on information obtained by Dr. John Rowe we collected material from the family of Sheikh Ssekimwanyi and from other *hajis* of long standing. Ali Kalumba's *Ebyafayo*, chapter 9, p. 18, and his *Olugendo lwe' Makka ne Madina* (Kampala: African Pilot Press, 1955) [The Journey to Mecca and Medina] are also relevant. Details can also be gleaned by looking through the *Uganda Gazette* from 1910 onwards. For large-scale pilgrimage by air see the local newspapers and magazines like *Al-Noor*, special number of March 1968 (Kampala: Sapoba Bookshop Press, Katwe).

6   Kalumba, *Ebyafayo*, 22-27, discusses the role of Muslims in the slave, ivory and gun trades in pre-colonial times and then goes on to speak of their work in running buses, fisheries, meat companies, food contracting, as well as motor and bicycle dealing and repairing.

was not paid by a Mission, but he was "a person sent" by Islam at large. In his life he showed forth his religion, attracted others to it, and helped them to learn, so far as he could.

A number of the "sub-imperialists," that is, Africans who joined in the task of bringing outlying areas under colonial government control, were Muslims. Their influence and activity is best illustrated by giving extracts from an interview between Abdu Kasozi and Hassan Ssebowa, who was reputed to be over a hundred years old:

Kasozi:
Mr. Ssebowa, you are old and you know many important things of the world. Tell us what you know and what you have seen in your life and why you are here.

Ssebowa:
I am an old man and I reached retiring age in 1922. I was one of the pages who served in Kabaka Mwanga's palace after the wars of religion. I was a Muslim and I used to follow the Kabaka here and there. When there were many fightings and killings, the European, Kapere Lugaadi [Captain Lugard] came and settled the land. The chiefs like Kagwa were friendly to the European, and the Kabaka was not very happy with them. But he was very friendly to his Mujaasi Gabriel [Commander of forces]. To show his friendship towards him above all others, Mwanga in public gave him a gun as a sign of friendship. But the chiefs were so annoyed that they decided to get that gun. Somehow it was stolen from Gabriel's house and found its way to Apolo Kagwa's house [Kagwa was a leading Protestant and Katikiro, or Prime Minister].

Gabriel came before the Kabaka and vowed revenge on the thief. He had heard that the gun was in Apolo Kagwa's house. Apolo's house was a double-storied one—let no one deceive you that the first two-storied house in Buganda was not built by Apolo Kagwa. When Gabriel heard that the gun was in Apolo Kagwa's he decided to go there. He waited till all the great chiefs, the Kabaka, and the important men were in council discussing affairs of state. He pretended to be ill and excused himself to be absent. In fact he went to the Katikiro's [Kagwa's] home instead of to the physician. He deceived the guards saying that the Katikiro had sent him to collect some very important documents in the bedroom. As the guards knew him as Gabriel, the Mujasi, they let him in. When, however, he delayed coming out, the guards got suspicious and followed him upstairs. He shot one of the guards, and the shots were heard even by the chiefs' council. There was chaos in the country. The Mujasi brought the gun and showed it to the Kabaka saying, "I am a man and I must die like a brave man; not like a woman. Here is your gun."

The country was in chaos. The Kabaka, due to his friendship with the Mujasi, rose in arms [against the whole set-up which limited his power and give it to men like Kagwa]. The Kabaka ran towards the lake. Many of us who were pages followed the Kabaka—as was our custom. We followed him to the lake, running. Those of us who were lucky got into boats and went to Sukuma [in Tanganyika]. We were now in a country ruled by the Dachi [Germans]. We, however, left that place and, passing through Koki, Kyaka, Kakuuto, Kibaali, Kibula, Isingiro, Igara, Mawogola, went into Bunyoro. By this time the Kabáka had a few followers. In Buddu [southwestern Buganda] there was a terrible war especially at Nyendo of those who supported Mwanga and those who did not. A few years later, many skulls could be seen.

Mwanga, however, was caught with Kabarega [King of Bunyoro]. The *Bazungu* [Europeans] wanted to restore Mwanga as Kabaka, but the chiefs like Apolo Kagwa refused. At this juncture all of us pages and faithful chiefs who were following Mwanga were left helpless in Bunyoro. We were, however, lined up for inspection by Nubians and Bazungu. Those who were fit were recruited into the army. For me, I was lucky. A British officer selected me as his servant. I followed my master wherever he was posted. He contributed much in starting towns and D.C.s' [District Commissioners'] stations like Masaka, Mbarara and others. Let no man deceive you. It was I, yes, I, Hassan Ssebowa, who built Mbarara. We came with many *Bazungu* [Europeans]. We did not know many of these *Bazungu*. They ate alone, slept alone, and played alone. We, the Blacks, also had our own quarters, our own food, and ate together. Ankole, at that time, was a very small country and we helped to enlarge it. There were many kings who lost their thrones to join Ankole. [The old gentleman gave details of this compulsory building up of the Ankole Kingdom and of border disputes between British, Belgians, and Germans. He then told of how he went to Egypt with his British employer as a personal servant. On his return he was recommended to the police force and helped to start police stations in many places. (His son said he began his police service in 1902 at Kabale). Eventually he was promoted to being a Gombolola (County) Chief and station agent in Kigezi and retired in 1920 to settle down locally and build up a comfortable and noble establishment].

Kasozi:

Did you have power to recruit and give jobs in government service to other people?

Ssebowa:

Oh yes. I did and I recruited many. I was the giver and taker. I was the best known African and all Bazungu knew me. Whoever I recommended as a chief was put in charge.

Kasozi:

Do you remember some of the people you selected and gave jobs?

Ssebowa:

Yes, but very many of them, very many, went back to Buganda.

Kasozi:

You are a Muslim, and it seems you recruited many Muslims as chiefs.

Ssebowa:

Naturally, one serves his own people first; when I got a suitable Muslim, I made him a chief. But I did not make useless ones chiefs.

Kasozi:

Do you remember some of their names?

Ssebowa:

Zakaria Bakare was made a Gombolola chief in Bufumbira; Arajabu Mwebe worked at Kamwezi Gombolola though he was not a Gombolola chief; and many others. But there were not many Muslims of good caliber.

Kasozi:
Did you come to Kigezi as a Muslim?

Ssebowa:
Yes, in fact I have told you already that I was a Muslim when I left Catholics, allowing them to build at Rugarama and Rushoroza.

Kasozi:
Did you do anything to the advantage of the Muslims?

Ssebowa:
Oh yes, I gave them the place to build the mosque at Kabale.

Kasozi:
Who was this man or group of people you helped in securing the mosque site at Kabale?

Ssebowa:
It was Amis - Amis Mzee, a Swahili. I cannot remember the date, but he was the man who started building it. I asked the government to give us that place. Because they knew me, it was very easy for me to get it.

Kasozi:
Did you help in the teaching or spreading of Islam in this area?

Ssebowa:
No, not directly, as I was a government servant. I had to serve all religions. However, I paid money for the Islamic religious teacher in that school for some time.

Kasozi:
Why are there many Muslims in Kinkizi?

Ssebowa:
Because there were Muslim rulers. Abdalla Namunye and Ntangamalalo were both Muslims. He built Mosques and religious schools for them.

Kasozi:
Did you do the same in the areas you ruled in?

Ssebowa:
No, as a ruler I had no clan, I had to serve all people.

Kasozi:
Who were the first Muslim religious leaders to come to Kigezi?

Ssebowa:
Rajabu Mwebe, Arajab Marigani. who was paid by government, Masoudi Mukasa, Amani and others.

Kasozi:
Do you remember the first Bakiga [men of Kigezi] to become Muslims?

Ssebowa:
> Asumani Kanyooma of Rujumbura whose son is in Kabale; Musa Rwakalala (whom I helped to be made a Muluka chief. He became a Muluka chief at Kabale with my recommendations); and Abdalla.

Kasozi:
> Who were the first traders in Kabale?

Ssebowa:
> These were Swahilis, Arabs and later, Indians.

Kasozi:
> What were their religions?

Ssebowa:
> They were Muslims though some Indians were Baniani [Hindu].[7]

From this material and a vast quantity of similar oral history of which only part has been recorded it is possible to gauge the tremendous achievements of the Ugandan Muslims of the first generations. But they are accused by their own young people of failure to grasp the key to entry into the modern world.

2. ISLAM AND WESTERN EDUCATION

On the matter of modern education for Muslims, many young Muslims condemn the colonial government, the Christian missionaries and their older generation for failing miserably.[8] It is said that more and more was entrusted to

7   The interview took place on Easter Saturday, 1970, at Karorwe village in Buchinda sub-county, Ndorwa, Kigezi. The dialogue translated from the tape has been condensed and many interesting details not relevant to our immediate purpose omitted. Katherine J. Parry, a teacher at Kigezi High School, helped to conduct the interview. Her research interest is in the Balokole, a revival Christian group; material relating to them follows the point where we have cut off our description.

8   Information about Muslim education in the colonial period is fairly copious. A good guide to sources will be found in Felice Carter, "The Education of African Muslims in Uganda," *Uganda Journal* 29 (1965), 193 ff., and J. Sykes, "A further note on the Education of African Muslims," 30 (1966), 227 ff. See also M. Musoke, "Muhammadan Education," *Uganda Teachers' Journal*, 1, No. 4 (1939), 242 f. and *Report by the Fact-Finding Mission to Study Muslim Education in East Africa*, (Nairobi, 1958). There is a good deal of general material in the Makerere Department and Institute of Education. Much oral information was obtained from Muslim students at Makerere and Kibuli and from Messrs. Ramadhani Gava, Ntege-Lugwama, L. Zake, and Abu Mayanja. See also David G. Scanlon, *Education in Uganda* (Washington: United States Office of Education, 1964) and his general books on education in Africa. (We owe this and other assistance on educational matters to Francis King's unpublished Certificate in Education thesis, "Religious Education in Uganda", Oxford, 1970.)

the missions; the British found this the cheapest and most effective way of providing education. But Muslims had no comparable organizations for most of the colonial period. In some cases colonial officials tried to insist on fair play, but too often the Christians stopped these efforst by saying this was to give the Muslims an advantage. Muslim teachers of good quality and integrity were hard to come by. Few Muslims could get teacher training. Some so-called Muslim teachers were Christians who had been dismissed for bad conduct; they had indeed joined Islam but had not reformed their own characters.

Beyond all this, so some informants say, the real difficulty was the hard core of African Muslim conservatism. The old men lived in another world, they did not want to be hurried into modern western society. They suspected European education which began by teaching children to read from left to right and went on with its running water to wash away respect for decent conduct from the heads of children.

It is necessary to go somewhat more deeply into this apathy or even antipathy towards western education, which, if it is true, means that the most important single factor in the situation holding up western education for Muslims was the Muslims themselves. To some people the necessity of western education is axiomatic; in fact, soon no one will be allowed to clean drains without a University degree. Yet Churchill, Washington, Muhammad had no such training. It is a piece of western arrogance to say that a young Muslim is illiterate if he cannot read English. The Sheikhs and *ulema* were suspicious of western education; not only was it tainted by being largely in Christian hands, but even in its "secular" form it had anti-Islamic connotations. For Muslim parents education is not only a matter of what subjects a child learns but what kind of man or woman it creates. Not everybody thinks western man and woman are worth emulating: indeed, some Ugandan Muslims thought Arab man and his women, as modified by Africa, were the ideal. Present-day young Ugandan Muslims insist that we must not confuse Islam with Arabness, but many of the older generation went that way.

The old men maintain theirs was not a bad way of life. Many of them were fairly rich, they had some Qur'anic education and could keep accounts. As butchers, transport and taxi drivers and owners, as farmers keeping cattle and growing cotton and coffee, they could marry young and live a good life, accumulating houses, land, wives, and children. Theirs was a full life, permeated and given dignity by religion. They were slow-moving indeed, but they gave a needful steadiness and balance in giddy times. Their thrift, hard work, and cautious innovation provided the country's economic development with a sound base.

This conservative view is not unattractive, especially if we consider it against the desire of modernizing groups who wish to rush onwards headlong into the world of science and technology without counting the cost. It is also necessary to remember the wistful questioning of many young African Christians who, after years of book learning, temporary celibacy, dependence on parents and scholarships, know they can go on to a frustrating white-collar job and even unemployment. A way of life which gives man fullness of being, riches and contentment, even though it does not educate him in western ways, is attractive in itself; it needs no defense nor hurried adaptation to the modern world.

The Muslim community put a good deal of effort into the traditional Qur'an school, the *madrasa*, which is called *madarasati* in Uganda. Formerly probably three-quarters of the Muslim children attended one, even if they ran away after a year or at some point went on to a western-type school run by the Christian missions or the government. At the present time it is possible that about half of Muslim children go to such schools. A child will learn something about the Arabic letters and the Qur'an from his father, then he will be taken to the school of a *mwalimu* (Swahili loan word for "teacher"), whose wife may well be running a similar school for girls. Often he actually lives with the teacher and learns the total Islamic way of life by example. His father will give the teacher regular gifts or payments as the lad progresses through the various stages.

The method of teaching is by imitation and rote, corporal punishment reinforces instruction. The teacher will write some words from the Qur'an and then the pupils will copy them on their writing-boards and sing-song the sounds. Thus *surah* after *surah* of the Qur'an is committed to memory and the pupil learns to be able to copy Arabic correctly. In some places he may go on to quite advanced levels in exegesis and jurisprudence.

An interesting collection of text books used in Ugandan Qur'anic schools has been made at Makerere. It includes "A primary Text called the ship of salvation of the principles of religion and jurisprudence by Sheikh, the learned, the excellent, Salim, son of Sumir of Hadramawt, according to the law school of Imam al-Shafi." This Sheikh was born in 1860-1861 and died after a long life in Jakarta in Indonesia. The three-cornered connection in Islamic learning between southeast Arabia, Indonesia, and East Africa, based on *dhow* traffic using the monsoon winds, still has its influence in Uganda. For instance, one of the greatest teachers of Islam in Uganda has been Sheikh Ahmad Taha al-Haddad al-Alawi of Hadramawt who studied in Indonesia and regularly traveled from Mombasa to the Congo, teaching and preaching.

Another text book in the Makerere collection is a hand-written work produced by an imaginative Ugandan teacher with his own illustrations and careful selection of Arabic words of increasing difficulty. This teacher, Abbas Zaid al-Asadi, said that some of the material was based on the lessons given by Sheikh Ali Zaki from Hadramawt who taught in Uganda for three years before going home.[9]

9   Both texts brought in to Makerere by Arye Oded in February 1968. Also
     see Ali Kulumba, *Empagi Z'Obusiramu mu Luganda* [The Pillars of Islam",
in Luganda] Kampala: Mengo Printers, (1953) on the five duties, and A. B. K.
Kasozi, "The influence of Koran Schools on the Education of African Muslims",
Dini na Mila, 4 (1970), 1-21. For a West African Muslim's view of Qur'an schools
see Cheikh Hamadou Kane, *Ambiguous Adventure* (French original, Paris:
Julliard, 1961; English translation, New York: Walker, 1963).

A number of young Muslims who have received a full western education do not look upon Qur'an schools with much nostalgia. They remember their suffering in them and blame them for diverting the resources and interest of the community from "proper" schools. All this is not to suggest that Islam in Uganda did not in the end come to terms with modern education. Muslim boys and girls in increasing numbers went through schools and colleges of Christian foundation, maintaining their faith. More and more the Christian authorities began to realize that their earlier policy of bringing every kind of pressure to bear to convert a Muslim when he was in a Christian school was "sheep stealing." Towards the end of the colonial period when on a number of occasions dinner conversations with the head teachers of Budo, Nyakasura, Gayaza, Nabumali and Mwiri was brought round to this topic, they gave the impression that they would be embarrassed by such a conversion if it took place at all and certainly if it was a result of any kind of underhand methods.[10]

At the same time the Muslims were developing a modern schools system which could receive government assistance. At Lukalu in Butambala County Juma Tomusange set up a Qur'an school in 1937. "Secular" subjects were grafted in and Government recognition obtained. Thanks largely to the efforts of Ramadhani Gava, a Uganda Muslims Education Association was started in 1940. Despite opposition from some of the Sheikhs the Association was successful and the colonial government gave it, from 1948 onwards, the kind of recognition it gave the Uganda Protestant and Catholic educational organizations. In 1963, that is, soon after Independence, the Ministry of Education implemented its policy of taking over direct control of education from the religious bodies while allowing them recognition for the work they had done and permitting them to assist in a number of ways still open to them. The U.M.E.A. had, between 1940 and 1963, most creditably assisted in promoting modern education for Muslims.

It is unfortunate that the full history of the Muslim educational complex on Kubuli hill in Kampala has not been written.[11] The land was given by Prince Badru. A mosque reminiscent of the Arabian Nights for beauty, especially among the mists of a Kampala dawn, crowns the hill. It was built as a result of the cooperation of Muslims of various types and racial backgrounds. A school was opened in 1922. In 1945 junior secondary classes were started and in 1960 a beginning was made with senior secondary work. Today it has full teaching, including the Natural Sciences, as far as University level. Its coeducational, academic and residential facilities make it one of the most advanced schools in the Muslim world. In 1954 Kasawo Teacher Training College was moved to Kibuli and trained teachers of quality began to become available. The colonial

---

10   These are the main long-established schools of Native Anglican and Church of Uganda background. Prince Badru himself attended Budo. Abdu Kasozi was at Nyakasura.

11   This gap has been filled on the sociology and economics of education side by Regina M. Solzbacher, "Kibuli", *Uganda Journal*, 33 (1969), 163-174.

government made senior officers and teachers available to help at Kibuli. Many of them were keen Christians who realized that they fulfilled their own religion by serving Muslims faithfully. In 1966, thanks to U.S.A.I.D., new buildings and staff houses were opened. U.N.E.S.C.O. and other international organizations have now for some years been sending experts in Islamics from such countries as Egypt. Al-Azhar, the ancient Mosque-University at Cairo has, with Egyptian government help, been sending personnel too. Ugandans who have been trained in Pakistan have come back to teach.

3. SOME UNEXPECTED ALLIES

Muslims from Cutch, Kathiawar, and Gujerat in India have sailed down the coast of East Africa with the monsoon winds for centuries. In the nineteenth century they came inland and in the 1890s found their way into Uganda. They were mainly small shopkeepers, arrangers and suppliers of caravans, pioneers in bringing up supplies by porter and then by rail. They became interested in the marketing side of the coffee- and cotton-growing industries. These Muslims were mainly Shia' of the Ismaili, Ithna-asheri and Daudi Bohra (Ismā'īlī, Ithnā'asharī, Dāwūdī Bohora) groups but they recognized the local African Sunnis as their fellows and employed them as drivers, porters, messengers, domestic servants, and shopassistants. Generally when a non-Muslim African showed an interest in their religion and asked to become a Muslim, they brought him to the Sunni faith. When asked why this was, answers varied. Some said there was the language difficulty; others, that theirs was an esoteric form of Islam, and it was best to start with the more straightforward. Yet others said that local Islam was Sunni, and they wanted to strengthen it.

In 1945 His Highness the late Aga Khan Sultan Muhammad at a conference in Mombasa to which representatives of Muslim groups from all over East Africa had been invited said that at the Judgment Day his hearers would be judged, not by their fasting or prayers, but by their reply to the question "What have you done to save Islam in East Africa?" He, who during his first visit to East Africa at the end of the nineteenth century had been alarmed by the news of Kalema's fall and the swallowing up of the Sultanate of Zanzibar by the colonial power, had lived to look forward to a new day in which Islam might come into her own. The Aga Khan and his followers gave generously in their agreement to match each locally given shilling with a donated shilling. They liberally assessed the value of lands and services given and matched them with money. They took care to unite all Muslims in the effort and to ensure that Ismailis did not corner the positions of power nor gain undeserved prominence. In many parts of Uganda mosques and schools have sprung up as a result of the efforts of this East African Muslim Welfare Association.

Sometimes when a particularly big project is opened to the public a printed souvenir is issued. Those for the Wandegeya Mosque and school in Kampala and the Mosque and school in Soroti are just two examples which tell an interesting story of cooperation between Muslims of different races and foretell a great future for East African Islam. The Association's finding of scholarships for impecunious students has also paid rich dividends, especially in regard to students in Ugandan Secondary Schools and Makerere. Students have also been sent to Egypt and Pakistan. The Association claimed that the number of Muslims in Uganda doubled in the first five years after its foundation in 1945. Certainly it has been a major factor in the modern progress of Islam.

The non-Shia Indo-Pakistani groups who have also helped should be mentioned. In Kampala and other large towns some Sunnis from the Punjab and Sind are usually to be found. They are men who have prospered mainly by selling cars and bicycles. They show brotherly friendship and hospitality to African Muslims and are meticulous in attending the local Friday mosque at the great festivals. They have done much to remind Pakistani Muslims of their duty towards African Islam. It is to be hoped that they will succeed in bringing more educational material and teachers from Pakistan to Africa.

The Ahmadiyya Muslim Mission started in the Punjab at Qadian but at partition in 1947 moved its headquarters to Rabwah in Pakistan.[12] They began work in Uganda in 1946 and have converted a number of people (some say two thousand, others say many more). Their main contribution has been to show Muslims how to use methods exploited so effectively by the Christians over the years. They are not afraid to call themselves missionaries and use missionary methods. Though no language other than Arabic can give the full glory and meaning of the Qur'an, they have translated portions into Luganda. Their fierce and no-holds-barred controversial methods with Christians are not liked by other Muslims any more than their way of turning Sunni Muslims into Ahmaddiyya, but their aggressive evangelism, thorough propaganda and genuine personal godliness wins the admiration of other Muslims and Christians alike.

Another element in the internal confluence of religious forces which together constitute Ugandan Islam is the Islam of the Nubians.[13] The Nubi were soldiers recruited in the Sudan by the Egyptian agents who, in the nineteenth century, pushed up the Nile towards the great lakes. When the Egyptian

12   The material given on the Ahmadiyya is based on interviews in English and Hindustani by Abdu Kasozi and Noel King with Maulvi Ahmed Sufi and other missionaries in 1967 and 1969. A welcome blaze of publicity was received when *Life* featured this Mission's work.

13   This material on the Nubians is based on field notes collected at Bombo by Azim Nanji in May 1966, by Abdu Kasozi during a two-month stay in 1967, and by Noel King during a series of visits in 1965 and 1967. Dr. Oliver Furley's "Sudanese Troops in Uganda", *African Affairs*, 58 (1959), 311-327, gives details and a map. The information on Sheikh Abdullah was provided by his son, Yasin Haji Mohamed. The Secretary of the Sudanese Association has a complete file on its transactions which he kindly put at our disposal. Mr. S. Doka also had a collection of poetry in "the Nubian language." We are also obliged to Sheikh Muhammad Lathu and other venerable Nubi gentlemen who on numerous occasions patiently discussed their religion and history with us.

dominion collapsed because of the Mahdi taking the Sudan, and Emin Pasha withdrew, the Nubian soldiers were left without a commander. Lord Lugard and other British officers took them over and used them in their campaigns. By this time they had grown used to living off the land and had accumulated thousands of women and other campfollowers. They served the British well, but under the conditions of hard campaigning, bad pay, heavy discipline, and forced marches a number rose in mutiny in 1897. They were put down with difficulty; luckily for the British, the African Muslims and the Indian troops remained loyal to the imperial power. The Nubian ringleaders were shot, and those implicated on a lower level dismissed from the service. A good number were not involved and were retained in the British service. Colonies of Nubians settled near Bombo, Hoima, and Entebbe, and from them promising yound men joined the King's African Rifles and police force. Sections of that famous regiment were important in· the army of independent Uganda, which recently took over the government of the country. It is possible that Muslims of Nubian background will play a great role in the affairs of Uganda.

The Nubians were originally of many tribes including the Madi and Shilluk but took as their own a *lingua franca* which included much Arabic as well as Nilotic elements. Islam was also received as part of their identity. Originally this was of the Maliki (Māliki) law-school, but almost imperceptably they have gone over to the Shafi (Shāfi'i) way, which the Swahili brought from the coast, on the principle of *taqlid*, accommodation of rules in order not to displease another party. For.instance, they have conformed to the much stricter Shafi rule about literally not touching a woman between the lesser ablution and prayer. Again, while they used to leave their arms unfolded in prayer, they now follow the coastal custom.

By the Nubi mosque at Bombo there is the grave of Sheikh Haji Muhammad Abdullah al-Barnawi, a northern Nigerian, who died in 1944. He went on the pilgrimage in the 1890s, lived at Mecca seven years, then went to Egypt for three and on to Ethiopia for seven. Thence he went to Kismayu in Somaliland and was recruited as a kind of teacher-chaplain. In 1905 he came to Kenya to do this work and visited Uganda. He also saw service in Tanganyika. In 1930 he returned to Uganda and then mainly taught at Bombo with regular long visits to Arua in West Nile. He is said to have converted thousands of Ugandans and to have taught a number of their leading Sheikhs.

A Sudanese Association was founded in 1946 to look after the interests of Nubi in Uganda. In 1947 it had a paid-up enrollment of over two thousand men. It started an educational, sports, and welfare program with Mr. S. Doka as General Secretary. It has been most successful in assisting its members and Muslim ex-servicemen in general to find work and to obtain an education for their children.

The Nubian community has served Islam in Uganda by being a Muslim "presence" in many places and walks of life. It has imparted the prestige of the military and of reliable people who can be trusted with responsibility; it has provided faithful Muslims who have known their religion and imparted it to others.

4.   "CLERICAL" LEADERSHIP AND TRAINING

There is no priesthood in Sunni Islam. Perhaps because of its continued proximity to Christianity, its womb-mate or cradle partner, Ugandan Islam is much more conscious than most forms of Islam of the need for a well-trained and active "clerical" leadership. The training, "ordaining" or "enturbanning" of Sheikhs is given much attention. It is commonly agreed that one of the first Ugandan Sheikhs was a certain Abdalla who may have had the additional name "Mayanja." He escaped during Mutesa's persecution in the 1870s with a caravan to Zanzibar. There he did well in his studies and returned to his home as a Sheikh. He is said to have assisted in the training of the country's two leading Sheikhs, Shuaib Ssemakula and Ahmed Nsambu, both of whom have now reached a venerable age and have been active in the training of others.

The life story of Sheikh Shuaib is interesting in itself and at the same time tells us a good deal about Ugandan Islam and its place in the religious life of the country.[14] He was born in 1879 in Busiro County of Buganda; his father was a Protestant, so he was brought up and educated as a Christian. He still loves and uses his Bible, for in fact it was the Christian Bible that pointed him to Islam. Also the brotherly love, mutual help, communal worship, and cleanliness of Muslims attracted him.

When he was sixteen, he went to Kisumu. There he found himself alone and had to learn Swahili. He joined a caravan of porters bringing things to Kampala and fell seriously ill on the way. It was some Swahili Muslims who rescued him and brought him home. It was now the time of the revolt of the Nubians (1897), and the Europeans had run away from the places on the route. The Swahili taught him the two *shahada* (the declaration that there is no God but Allah and Muhammad is his prophet). After things had settled down he meditated much on religion. He felt that he had accepted the declaration out of fear but at the same time he wanted to be a good Muslim and to know more about Islam. He and his brother went to find the Muslims at Entebbe and arrived at the time of the noon prayer and asked to be initiated. "The *mwalimu* had not got things prepared but we insisted and we sharpened a little knife during the prayer and after it we were circumcized."

Even so he desired knowledge. He went to the Katambala, Mr. Magato, who gave him a little land and then found a certain District Commissioner's cook who was a *mwalimu* (teacher). "He baptized me after teaching me the

---

14   Sheikh Shuaib kindly put at our disposal two autobiographical notebooks
     written down by his son Sheikh Muhammad Katende which were
     translated by Samuel Busulwa and J. E. Nsubuga. Abdu Kasozi is preparing an
     edition of the original for publication as well as an article on "The *Maulidi* in
     Uganda" which is to appear in *Dini na Mila*, a journal published by the
     Department of Religious Studies and Philosophy at Makerere. The Sheikh also
     generously granted us a number of interviews in which we went over his
     autobiography and made recordings. The material given is based on the
     notebooks, but direct quotations from the tape are included.

fundamentals of the faith, and as he poured the water on me and I was washing, he repeated many words and gave me my name, Shuaib."[15]

He studied further and read the Qur'an in nine months. He began to teach new converts. Though he had just married a wife he went off to Tanganyika to study yet more. Then Bwana Nuhu Mbogo confirmed him as an assistant *mwalimu* who led the *juma* prayer at the Mosque at Mmende, built at the tomb of Ssekabaka Kalema. He later became Iman at a Mosque in Kyaddondo.

Still seeking knowledge he found a Sheikh in Mbale (Eastern Province) and studied there. He and his teacher traveled together teaching. Whenever they rested beneath a tree or in a house, the Sheikh asked him to read some text book and then he would comment. He saw the great famine and plague. He fought against false divination and played his part in the *juma-Zuhuri* dispute. In the end he was ready to accept almost any reasonable proposals, for to him the unity of Islam was of more importance than one or two prayers.

Sheikh Shuaib was one of those who helped to popularize the *mawlidi*, a service of Qur'an recitation, chants in honor of the prophet, and general jubilation. Though some said there could be no drumming in Islam (a ruling sufficient to break any African's heart unless he were a Puritan), the Sheikh allowed the small *matali* drums and tambourines, for there was a tradition that the Prophet himself had been welcomed with them.

In 1933 he registered his group with a Qur'anic title - *Jamiat el Islam*. Busily he set to work organizing schools and getting them up to a standard where parents could be proud of them and government recognize them and subsidize them. Another of his great interests was the training and ordaining of Sheikhs. He set a high standard both in learning and in morals.

It would not be amiss to remark that Sheikh Ssemakula has nothing but love and respect for the Christianity which had pointed him forward to Islam and he was not prepared to let the Christians stand alone when it came to education and high quality training for the ministry. One day in 1965 when we went to his house to continue our recordings, we found a choir of small boys with a Sheikh chanting *Surah Ya Sin* and we too were admitted and we prayed for our friend and teacher, for we were assured he was dying. They took him to the great modern hospital, and there he lay for months on the edge of death. But suddenly he recovered and continues rushing from place to place, building up Islam. He recognized the newly formed National Association for the Advancement of Muslims (felicitously abbreviated to N.A.A.M., the Arabic for "yes," which we shall mention later on).

As the colonial period drew to its end, educated Ugandan Muslims were

---

15 The use of baptism with name-giving may indeed be under Christian
    influence. But in coastal Swahili circumstances where many converts are
  already circumcized under tribal custom, the ritual bath with its cleansing from
  the impurity of "gentile" life attains prominence, though it is generally agreed
  that it is the declaration of witness to Allah and his Prophet that makes a person
  a Muslim.

deeply dissatisfied with the lack of western education which they felt characterized their community and the colonial treatment of them. It is said that they had only one University graduate in 1962 when Britain handed over power. Yet in many other respects they had reason to be proud of their achievements.[16] They had penetrated into every part of the country and were expanding at a rate proportionately greater than any of the other religious groups. A firm and solid foundation for future expansion in numbers, in quality, and into every facet of the nation's life had been laid. The outlook was altogether different from the somber gloom into which Ugandan Islam had entered at the beginning of the colonial period. Before describing briefly the condition of things in the years since independence and summing up with regard to the interaction of Christianity and the Traditional Religions with Islam, it is necessary to go back to the beginning of the colonial period to fill in some details about Islam in some areas of Uganda outside Buganda.

16   For a detailed description of the interaction of the religions in matters of politics in the last decade before Independence, see F. B. Welbourn, *Religion and Politics in Uganda,* 1952-1962 (Nairobi: East African Publishing House, 1965).

CHAPTER III

A Glance At Some Other Areas

1. BUSOGA

Busoga is the district lying to the east of Buganda.[1] To its east lies the great lake and it is in Busoga that the young Nile leaves the lake to begin its long journey to the Mediterranean. The natural main line of communication between southern and central Uganda and the east coast runs through Busoga, but during a great part of the last century the Maasai lay across the Kenyan side of it. Few dared use the direct route from the coast around Mombasa to the Lake because of the terror their warriors inspired. In addition, the Baganda looked upon Busoga as their back door and believed their conquerors would enter that way. That was one of the reasons why in 1885 Kabaka Mwanga had Bishop Hannington speared to death in Busoga as he tried to come to Buganda from the northeast.

The first Muslims to enter Busoga were Arabs who came by this route probably early in the reign of Mutesa. They did not leave any permanent mark. Certain Muslims in the armies of Mutesa also came this way, but the first lasting work was done by African Muslims who had fled from Mutesa's persecution in the middle 1870s. Some of Mutesa's pages had originally come from Busoga; at court they had been attracted to Islam, and when the pages were scattered abroad by persecution, they made their way home.

The wars of religion and the first colonial settlement also had the effect of causing Muslims who had lived in Buganda to go elsewhere. Either they were disappointed and defeated men who wanted a new place in which to succeed or they came as assistants to Baganda sub-imperialists or to British colonial officers. One of these was Ali Lwanga who came to the Bulamogi area in Busoga. He was a man of many skills; he was an expert in Swahili (which might have become the *lingua franca* of Uganda had not the Christian missionaries of the second wave insisted that it was too Islamic and substituted Luganda), he knew how to make soap, and to cook new Arab and Swahili dishes. He was an interpreter for the

1   Busoga has attracted the special attention of Dr. Lloyd Fallers of Chicago, whose series of studies culminating in *Law Without Precedent* (Chicago: The University Press, 1969) should be consulted. Y. K. Lubogo's *History of Busoga* (Jinja: East African Literature Bureau, 1960) is unfortunately difficult of access outside Uganda. The information given on this section is largely based on field work carried out by Abdu Kasozi in 1969. Notes on field visits by Arye Oded in 1967 and 1968, and by Noel King with Martin Mbwana in 1966 have also been used. Reverend Cyprian Bamwoze, himself a Musoga with some Muslim antecedents, has interviewed a good number of pioneer Muslims and assisted with this section.

District Commissioner, then a county chief. As such he set up a fine household with local wives and daily general distribution of food.

Ali was not alone, for at the turn of the century both the Church Missionary Society and the government became alarmed at the speed with which Muslim power in Busoga was increasing. In 1896 Munulo became the Menya, or hereditary chief of Bugweri county. It was a royal position which was connected with the ancient kingship of Bunyoro and held the highest prestige. Soon after his accession he was circumcized by Yusufu Luzige, a Muslim from Buganda. It is said that one of his motives was to escape from power of the traditionalists at his court, his numerous "uncles" and other relatives who would normally share the exercise of power. He insisted that all those who were on his side should become Muslims and brought pressure to bear on those who held back. In his *jihad* he defeated his opponents, who were either themselves circumcized or handed over their sons for the operation.

The British District Officer discovered what Munulo was doing and punished him as well as the interpreter who had given Munulo the impression that the European would not disapprove of his warfare on his relatives. At this point (1897) the Nubians mutinied and released Munulo from prison. After the Mutineers had been put down, Munulo refused to forsake Islam which had come under suspicion with the colonial power because of the recent uprising in which Muslims had killed British officers and a missionary. Munulo lost his throne and was exiled. In his own belief and that of many Basoga, he had suffered for his faith and had been unjustly treated by the foreigners. The people who had been coerced by Munulo into Islam remained in it and others joined them. Today Bugweri is one of the most solidly Muslim areas in eastern Uganda. On a Friday morning the roads are crowded with people in glistening white clothes going to the mosque.

Correspondence in the Entebbe archives reveals that the colonial officials in Busoga and the missionaries remained sensitive to Muslim activities for some time after the Nubian mutiny.[2] During the rest of the colonial period the Muslims of Busoga experienced the same difficulties with a school system largely in Christian hands, with a colonial government which at some levels gave Christianity an advantage while enabling Islam to go ahead at a good pace in the village and the commercial centers. Since World War II they have also had timely help from the Asian Muslims of the East African Muslim Welfare Association.

The effect on religion of a member of features unique to Busoga deserve special study. One is the effect of the enormous sugar plantations with their settlements for migrant laborers. Another is the sudden and planned industrialization and urbanization at Jinja based on the Owen Falls hydro-electric scheme. There is copper smelting with the Metal being brought in from Kilembe mine by rail; a nascent steel and iron industry; a bulb and lamp factory; a textile mill and other evidence of rapid industrialization and its accompanying social and religious

2   For instance, Busoga Correspondence, Outward, A11/1/53, 1900-1901 (cited above, compare item 55). Also see Inward, A10/1,2/43.

change. Islam is playing an increasing part in all this, but it is as yet impossible to define its role adequately.[3]

2.   BUKEDI, TESO, AND KARAMOJA

Bukedi is the district to the northeast of Busoga; formerly the term included the areas called Bugisu, Sebei, and Teso.[4] It is probable that the first Muslims to enter the area were Swahili traders during the last decades of the nineteenth century. During the period 1899-1902 Baganda soldiers were conquering the area in a form of sub-imperialism which was eventually replaced by British rule. The warlord Kakungulu had come out of Buganda to carve out a kind of kingdom for himself. A number of his followers were Baganda Muslims who had been disappointed by the turn of affairs in their homeland. When the British bureaucratized his royalist regime in the years following 1902, a number of these Muslims were appointed government agents. These included, for instance, Jafali Mayanja in south Bugisu, Sale Lule in north Bugisu and Abudale Makubire in Bunyole. Salimini Damulira served under the first and was still alive in 1968 at Lwakhakha in that district, while Salimu Mbogo served under the second and was still alive at Kachumbala in Teso. Up till that time their remembrances of the early history of Islam had not been recorded.

In 1911 the Acting District Commissioner sent a list of Baganda Agents to the Provincial Commissioner, Eastern Province. About half the names are Islamic, and the retainers of these men were estimated to be one hundred and four.[5] These were all men who would have wives, servants, and dependents.

Kakungulu and the British opened up communications: Arab, Swahili, and Asian traders of Muslim background came in and settled. They employed local Africans whom they encouraged to become Muslim. Sheikh Kale bin Shale who is the *mwalimu* of the chief Sunni mosque in Mbale came to the place in 1906 as an ivory trader and remained on as a teacher. The Adatia family is an example on the Ismaili side, the family of Hassanali on the Ithna-asheri, of Asian Muslims

---

3   C. And R. Sofer, *Jinja Transformed* (Kampala: East African Institute of Social Research, 1955) have not been sufficiently followed up from this point of view.

4   The material given is based on field visits by the three writers and on notes contributed by Dr. Michael Twaddle, formerly of Makerere, now of the London School of Oriental and African Studies. Dr. Twaddle should not be held responsible for the manner of presentation nor for errors of fact which may have crept into this account. His article, "The Founding of Mbale," *Uganda Journal*, 30 (1966), 25-38, also bears on our topic. The area is a bottle-neck in the migration corridor along the Nile towards the great lake and the fair lands beyond. Ethnology is complicated, for Bantu, Nilotic, and Nilo-Hamite elements intermix.

5   W. G. Adams, 11 September 1911, Entebbe Archives S.M.P. 519/1909.

who came as shopkeepers and pioneers of motor transport and spread Muslim influence by giving help of various kinds including money to local mosques and schools.

Another wave of Muslim influence from Buganda came from around 1914 when "The Missionary Committee" (*kakiko k'emisane*) of the Muslims at Kibuli Mosque at Kampala sent about six Baganda religious teachers to Bukedi. At least one of them, Sowedi Namusanga, was still alive and residing in the area in 1968. If this was a regular Committee, possibly the Muslim Baganda were as missionary minded as their Christian brethren who are outstanding in Africa (and perhaps the world) for sending out missionaries within a few years of their own conversion. (Even that miracle, the Anglo-Saxon Church, needed longer between St. Augustine coming to Canterbury and the sending of Boniface to Germany.)

The results of the work of these Baganda were spectacular. The Christians took alarm, especially as some of the tribes here were amongst the few in Uganda which practice circumcision as a tribal custom. However the rate of increase does not seem to have been sustained. Only in the last decade has it reached and passed the levels of the early years.

To the northwest of Bukedi lies Teso.[6] The people are mainly cattle-keeping Nilo-Hamites who differ considerably from the banana-growing Bantu of the areas to the southeast. Till around 1901 they were lumped together with the other tribes as *Bakedi*. In Luganda, if this was pronounced *Bakeedi*, it could mean "naked ones," which was a true description as far as it went, but did not indicate the great differences of language, social and political structure and religious outlook. The fighting connected with the British and Ganda campaigns in the war on Omukama Kabarega and Kabaka Mwanga and the revolt of the Nubians was fought partly across this area. Kakungulu invaded and "pacified" Teso. He forbad their gatherings for initiations and interfered with the age-set system. His followers helped themselves to the women, whose tall, slim beauty was greatly appreciated, and to the cattle. As the British took over from Kakungulu, they and the Christian missionaries who came with them, or even preceded them, were concerned to "civilize" the people and bring them nearer to the standards of the Baganda. Roads were opened up, and cotton as a cash crop introduced. The trade in cattle flourished.[7]

In the late nineteenth century Arab and Swahili traders in search of ivory as well as Muslim Baganda traveling because of war or diplomacy and Muslims in the Egyptian service passed through Teso. When colonialism opened up the country Swahili, Arab, and Indian Muslim traders came in and settled. A good

6   On Teso see J. C. D. Lawrance, *The Iteso* (London: Oxford University Press, 1957) and Pamela and P. H. Gulliver, *The Central Nilo-Hamites* (London: International African Institute, 1953, rpt. 1968).

7   The unpublished Ph.D. thesis of M. Louise Pirouet, *The Expansion of the Church of Uganda (N.A.C.) from Buganda into Northern and Western Uganda between 1891 and 1914*, University of East Africa, Makerere, 1968, has been of great assistance to the writers.

many of the Baganda lower officials brought in by Kakungulu and the British were Muslims.[8] On the surface it looks as if it should have been possible for Islam to take root and spread, but to judge by the figures of the 1959 census, the response was small. A good deal of further field research will be necessary before a satisfactory explanation is reached.

To the north of Bukedi lies Karamoja.[9] There were too few Muslims there to make statistical showing. Somali, Swahili, and Asian Muslim traders and settlers have been in that area since early in this century. The indigenous people are nomad pastoralists who apparently have not been affected by Islam. The apparent lack of impact on the people as a whole deserves closer study. At the same time Christians Missions, whether that of the Verona Fathers or the Bible Churchmen's Mission Society, did not do well either till fairly recently. A letter from the Provincial Commissioner to the Chief Secretary dated 30th November 1923 makes interesting reading:

> . . . the time has now arrived at which, in my opinion, the entry of Missions into Karamoja should be permitted.
>
> The district and people have now been well surveyed and the work of missions would be advantageous in all respects.
>
> There is, moreover, a very strong Mohammedan influence in the District which needs some counter influence. All the five agents, all the shopkeepers, and the first class Sergeant of the Uganda Police Unit are all Mohammedans and to prevent all the chiefs becoming proselytised, I consider that the District should be opened to other missionary influence.[10]

3.   ACHOLI, LANGO, AND WEST NILE

To the east of Karamoja lie Acholi and Lango. The statistics show a negligible Muslim population.[11]

Lango had come within the area affected by the raids carried out by Samuel Baker's and Emin Pasha's troops and the troubles over Mwanga and

8   At the Entebbe Archives it is possible to inspect the lists of agents discharged in given areas in certain years. Half of those discharged from service in Teso in 1914 had Islamic names.

9   The ethnographical survey by the Gullivers mentioned above covers Karamoja. Dr. P. H. Gulliver's work on the Jie and Maasai should also be consulted. In addition see P. T. W. Baxter's "Acceptance and Rejection of Islam among the Boran of the Northern Frontier District of Kenya" in ed. I. M. Lewis, *Islam in Tropical Africa* (London: Oxford University Press, 1966).

10   Entebbe Archives, S.M.P. 1307/1908, Karamoja. Information like this and the unmistakable Muslim presence, apparent on Noel King's field visits (for other purposes) in 1963 and 1967, belie the value of census figures. However, statistics cannot lie.

11   For a guide to the ethnographic background see Audrey Butt, *The Nilotes*

Kabarega as well as the revolt of the Nubians which we mentioned earlier. Survivors of the last helped some local people to carry out raids on chiefs in Lango and Acholi who had submitted to British rule. These raiders had to be put down by force in 1901. Even after that it was some time before the country was able to be pacified by the colonial power and effective control established. Gradually roads were built and in 1912 Lira was selected as the capital.[12]

Muslim Asians, Arabs and Swahili moved in to trade as the country was opened up. They married local women, and care had to be taken that these marriages were properly registered and the women's rights under Muslim law safeguarded by the colonial power.[13]

Once again Baganda agents, some of whom were Muslim, were used in Lango in the early colonial days before World War I; again Muslims did not set up schools in the Christian way till after World War II when money and encouragement given by the East African Muslim Welfare Association had its effects, but Muslims prospered in various trades, in the Police and similar roles. Though the external factors were much the same as in Buganda, the response to Islam before 1960 was small. The explanation for this has yet to be worked out; it has to do perhaps with the devastation of the country in the 1890s, with the social and political structure of the Langi, who did not have the large-scale organization of the kingdoms further south, and with their religion.

Acholi is the area bounded by the Sudan border in the north and in the south and west by the right angle of the Nile as it flows westward into Lake Albert and then northward out of it. The people are mainly Nilotic, part of the Lwoo migration out from their primordial fatherland along the river towards the

of the Sudan and Uganda. Also see F. K. Girling, The Acholi of Uganda (London: Her Majesty's Stationery Office, 1960) and T. T. S. Hayley, The Anatomy of Lango Religion and Groups (Cambridge: The University Press, 1947). J. H. Driberg, The Lango (London: T. Fisher Unwin, 1923) is still useful, though it says little about Islam. (It is whispered in Entebbe that Driberg was the mysterious British official who became a Muslim, but that too needs more research!) On the Traditional Religion, see articles by p'Bitek Okot in the Uganda Journal on jok, 27 (1963), 15-29, and on Fate, 29 (1965), 85-94. On the jogi also see King, Religions of Africa, 28-31. The Alur, some of whom live in Uganda, are a similar people and have been studied by Aidan Southall, whose The Alur (Cambridge: Heffer's for East African Institute of Social Research, 1956) sheds sidelights on the Acholi. A fuller book list will be found on p. 107 of King's Religions of Africa.

12   On the Lango Field Force of 1901 see Entebbe Archives, Shuli (Acholi) A16, II. The names of the mutineers are mainly Islamic, but so were most of the non-commissioned officers used by the British. On Lira see Eastern Province Annual Report, 1912, 703C.

13   Hamis bin Awaz, who was in charge of a mosque that was being built, was made a Deputy Registrar under the Mohammedan Marriage and Divorce Ordinance of 1906 (Acting District Commissioner at Kaberamaido, Lango, to Registrar General, Entebbe, 4 and 5 March 1914, M.P. 99/1914).

great lakes. Though the Acholi gave some traits of kingship to Bunyoro, they are not themselves organized into large kingdoms; each *Rwot* rules a fairly small area and often his authority is over one clan. In religion again the Acholi do not seem to have a clear concept of a supreme God. Divine phenomena are associated with spirits called *jogi* (plural of *jok*). When this explanation fails, they appear to fall back on a concept not unlike the Greek idea of Fate.

When Samuel Baker came up to Acholi in the 1870s, he found the country had been devastated by Khartoum slave traders. Emin Pasha brought some peace to the area but after his departure his Nubian troops lived off the land till some of them joined Lugard in 1891. Others went on with their raiding and were with difficulty brought under control. Settled colonial rule took some time to establish in Acholi. Christian missions suffered some severe setbacks, though they had some heroically devoted African workers from Alurland and Bunyoro. Their breakthrough came with the schools where they could insulate and teach the children and when they abandoned methods learnt in Buganda where the structure of society was radically different from that of Acholi. It remains for research to reveal the detailed course of Islam in Acholi and the reasons for the apparent lack of response. Perhaps the Acholi would not respond to the fiery Islam which came up the Nile and were too far from the gentle and attractive Islam brought from the Indian Ocean.

West Nile and Madi which lie to the east of Acholi are of great interest to us because of the large Muslim population in the Aringa County of West Nile (said to be around eighty percent) and in Madi. Unfortunately it was only possible to pay short visits there and it was impossible to find a Muslim student from there who was studying at Makerere and would help with long term research.

The area has been under strong Muslim influence ever since the Egyptians began extending their sphere of influence up to this part of the Nile in the 1870s. According to Haji Yusufu Nuhu, the Assistant Qadi of West Nile, Islam was brought to the area by soldiers serving under Baker, Gordon, and Emin.[14] Later, when the British took over the administration, they recruited soldiers from Aringa. When these local soldiers joined the government troops, who were mainly Sudanese and Muslim, they were converted. When they came back to Aringa, they taught Islam. A good example of such a soldier is Fadil Mulla Ali. He was a pagan when he was recruited but was converted later. When he retired he was made county chief of Aringa. He carried out a massive campaign to convert people to Islam and in this he was most successful. Others include Bilal Fadijala, Adam Bamasako, and Fadimulla Malijan who became a subcounty chief and converted many to Islam. To see holders of such officers professing Islam must have made the religion honorable in the eyes of the people.

Islam in Aringa spread more widely when Nubian soldiers began to settle

14   Interview with Abdu Kasozi 9 April 1968 and Noel King on 11 April. Most
      of the material given is based on a field visit in April 1968 and the present
      tenses refer to that time.

in West Nile, but especially when Sheikh Muhammad Abdallah from Bornu in Northern Nigeria, whom we mentioned in connection with Bombo, was made Qadi of West Nile. He taught Islam and though he lived at Arua he went to Aringa often to teach Islam there. He did not do any other work beside teaching. He stayed in West Nile for nine years before he moved to Bombo. Islamic knowledge in West Nile owes much to his work, for neither coastal nor Baganda Sheikhs went to West Nile in the early days.

The fact that no preachers came from the coast and Buganda probably explains why the type of Islami in West Nile was mainly Māliki and not Shāfi'i. In past years the Māliki faith became so entrenched that Sheikh Muhammad Galawan from Lamu who tried to change the state of affairs was not well received. He moved to Rhino Camp and became a trader. But Ahmad Khalifan, a prominent Muslim trader in Aruz, believes that the Māliki sect is decreasing because no preachers come from the north. Instead, West Nile is looking towards Kampala and the east from where her present preachers come. The result is that people professing the Māliki faith are now about sixty percent of the Muslims of West Nile.

In Arua town there are at least five big mosques. The Qadi of the main mosque is Juma Oba. It is under the influence of Haji Ramadhan who supports the authorities at Kibuli. Most of the people who pray at this mosque are Shāfi'i. The second mosque is found in the Tanganyika section of Arua. The Qadi here is Mwalimu Juma Malijan. It is here that Sheikh Muhammad Abdalla (the Nigerian) had his headquarters, and Malijan is his staunch follower. This mosque is probably the most purely Maliki mosque in Arua. Everyone prays with unfolded arms. The third mosque is at Awadiri on the Pakwach road built by the people of the area for convenience since almost all the other mosques are on the opposite side of Arua. The fourth mosque is the Aga Kahn one. Finally there is the Ithna-asheri mosque which is, in fact, very large. Such a large number of mosques in so small a town is probably an indication of how Islam has entrenched itself in the area.

Religious education in West Nile is given through *Madarasatis* (Qur'an schools) found all over the district. Some of these are like any other schools, but many are conducted in the shade of trees and on the verandas of houses. In the main *Madarasati* in Aura there are two Swahili Sheikhs recruited from Mombasa. No secular or English education is taught in this school, all the lessons are conducted in Arabic. At Yumbe, the biggest town in Aringa, there is also a *Madarasati.*

As far as western education is concerned, the Muslims of West Nile have recently (1967) been trying their best to send their children to good quality schools teaching modern subjects. The Headmaster of Geya Muslim School at Yumbe has to send away children because the classes are too full to contain all the pupils who want to join. About seven other Muslim primary schools face the same problem. A private senior secondary school under Amis Marijani at Geya has been opened up. Some Muslims complain that in the past the government has listened too readily to Christians who alleged that Muslims did not want to send their children to school. They said that this was calculated to keep Muslims backward and unfortunately the government had, in former days, listened to such nonsense. They had not given a senior secondary school to the Muslims, although they were the majority in the district.

The Muslims in West Nile complain of many difficulties. It is the belief of the majority of them that Islam is on the decline. This is because they have few qualified religious teachers of their own; though there are many Muslims in the area, there was not a single indigenous Sheikh in the district in 1968. Kampala, despite repeated requests from West Nile, had failed to send the religious teachers requested. Muslim children are being attracted by Christian missionaries who can provide not only education but medical care for both young and old. The leading Sheikhs of Kampala do not often visit West Nile to strengthen Islam as they do in other parts of Uganda. Financial help to complete mosques is also needed in West Nile.

Much research remains to be done on Islam in West Nile. The writers deeply regret that they had not been able to make even a beginning of detailed research on Islam among the Madi in 1968. These people number about 63,000 on the Uganda side of the border and live on both sides of the White Nile as it leaves Uganda for the Sudan. The Madi have responded in good number to Islam, though the Lugbara, who are closely related to them, have been apparently somewhat more resistant to it.[15]

4. THE KINGDOM OF BUNYORO

To the northwest of Buganda lay the kingdom of Bunyoro. It claimed to be the senior kingdom in the inter-lacustrine basin. Some of its ceremonies of sacral kingship have resemblance to those of the Pharoahs of Ancient Egypt.[16]

As we saw earlier, the Egyptian thrust up the River Nile started quite early in the nineteenth century. Raiding parties recruiting slaves for the Khartoumers had found their way into Bunyoro in the 1860s, and Samuel Baker came there in 1864. These men brought some Muslim influence, but of a kind which produced adverse reactions. The rulers of Bunyoro were as sensitive to Egyptian domination and anything that went with it as their counterparts in Buganda.

15 On the Lugbara, J. F. M. Middleton's *Lugbara Religion* (London: International African Institute, 1960) is a classic. His "Notes on the Political Organization of the Madi", *African Studies*, 14, No. 1, 29-36 remains one of the few easily accessible works on the Madi.

16 On Bunyoro see John Beattie, *Bunyoro, an African Kingdom* (New York: Holt, Rinehart & Winston, 1960), and A. R. Dunbar, *A History of Bunyoro-Kitara* (Oxford and Nairobi: Oxford University Press, 1965, rev. ed. 1969) and *Omukama Chwa II Kabarega,* (Kampala: East African Literature Bureau, 1965). Mrs. Ruth Fisher's *Twilight Tales of the Black Baganda* (London: Marshall Brothers, 1911) was misnamed by the publisher and mainly gives Toro legends and myths which often go back to Nyoro sources.

Some Arab and Swahili traders from the southeast found their way into Bunyoro early in the reign of Omukama Kabarega (1869-1899), the King who so staunchly resisted Samuel Baker and then Gordon's efforts to bring Bunyoro into the Egyptian dominion.[17] The Omukama was keen to obtain the firearms and gunpowder the traders could bring; neither he nor they seem to have paid much attention to propagating Islam. First the Baganda and then the British did their best to see that this line of communication was broken. Certainly few Banyoro at this time seem to have come to Islam because of direct contact with Swahili and Arab Muslims.

As mentioned earlier, in the days when Kabaka Mutesa was enthusiastic about Islam he sent a "mission" to Bunyoro. In describing this effort, Hamu Mukasa says:

> When the religion of the Muslims increased more and more, the Kabaka sent the following message to his brother Kabarega, the King of Bunyoro: 'My brother, I have sent you these two teachers, whose names are: Sabaddu, who was *mujasi* [commander of the forces], when he was still *musenero* [brewer], and Mwanga Sabakaki, to teach you the good words of God (Allah) who is greater than all the spirits and who governs heaven and earth and that the end will come when all men will be judged. I therefore do not like you, my brother, to be among those who will be condemned on that day of judgement.'
>
> Kabarega dismissed the people sent to him with this message: 'Go back and tell my brother who has sent you to teach me that I do not like the message he has sent me. I have my *lubaale* [spirit] who is my God. I do not fear the end he has told me of, neither does the fire that will burn those who refuse to obey God terrify me, for it will burn me only after death, in which case it will burn my bones only, when I no longer feel the pain. That is why I do not believe such talk. Besides, I have heard that people will rise again from the dead and be alive as they were before. Why, then, does the Kabaka of Bugaɴ... rejoice in such rising? Does he think it is true people will rise from the dead? Will he then continue to be Kabaka when his cruel father Suna whom he succeeded rises? Will he [Suna] not kill him? Let him know that when kings who ruled before him rise, he himself will become a common man. He must know that when his fellow princes rise too, they will inevitably fight him for having killed them without cause. He will have a hard time with the former kings and with his brothers whom he killed. I therefore pity him for his ignorance, that he rejoices over what will make him miserable, mistaking it for happiness. As for myself, I do not like to become a common man when my father Kamulasi [Lunyoro, Kamurasi] returns to be king after rising from the dead. After all, in this country of ours, we do not kill princes as it is done in Buganda. Therefore you who have come to teach me go back and tell him all this. Let his gifts too, the kettle and mat for praying and the flag to be put up on the pole on the Juma day, be returned to him. Over here I have my spirits who advise me concerning the affairs of my reign and my life. These are enough for me.[18]

17   G. Schweinfurth, F. Ratzel, R. Felkin, and G. Hartlaub, *Emin Pasha in Central Africa* (London, 1888), 114-123.

18   Mukasa, *Simudda Nyuma*, 14-17 (partly cited above). From this point to

During the rest of the reign of the great Omukama, Islam made little progress in Bunyoro. During the wars of religion in Buganda, especially when Kabaka Kalema came to Kijungute, some Banyoro were converted and in due time returned to their own country and taught Islam. A few Nubi, descendants of Emin Pasha's troops, settled in Bunyoro in the days when the King's African Rifles were stationed at Hoima. The company was withdrawn in 1911, so the Nubi did not remain for long. Thus the Nubian influence of the Maliki school is virtually absent.

In 1911 *Omubito* (prince) Aramanzane Mwirumubi, a son of Kabarega and brother to the *Abakama* (kings) Kitahimbwa, Duhaga II, and Winyi IV, was chosen as leader of the Banyoro Muslims. They were granted one square mile of freehold land in Bunyoro, but this was never demarcated because of lack of organization. The Banyoro Muslims relied on Buganda for help but did not obtain it. They remained a minority.

Up to about 1930 the Banyoro Muslims, like Muslims elsewhere in Uganda, tended to refuse to let their children go to non-Muslim schools. Since they lacked generous supporters abroad they were unable to found and maintain schools of sufficiently high standard to permit their students to compete successfully with pupils from Catholic or Protestant schools. Lack of modern educational facilities is fundamental to the past failure of Islam in Bunyoro to gain numbers. This even meant that the more able children of Muslim parents frequently were educated at Christian schools, were tempted to become Christians, and were lost from the Muslim community. For instance, Mohamedi Byamboijana, guardian of Kabarega's tomb, had four children by his wife Fatuma Tibahwerayo - Zaima Nyabatwa, George Mpabaisi, Alice Kyahurwa, and Yusufu Bagutatira. George, a transport contractor and progressive farmer, and Alice, an English-speaking domestic servant, started their education at a Muslim school but transferred to a Protestant school. They have achieved a higher education than have Zaina and Yusufu who were only educated at a Muslim school.

The following table further illustrates this point:

Schools in Bunyoro in 1932

	Central	Middle	Technical	Elementary Vernacular
Church Missionary Society	2	1	1	5
White Fathers' Mission	1	1	–	5
Muslim	–	–	–	1

the end of the section on Bunyoro, material supplied by A. R. Dunbar in 1967 has been used. It has not been updated but has had to be shortened and adapted to the shape of our other material, and in doing so we may have twisted it. Mr. Dunbar acknowledges help from the following, but does not wish them to

At this time education was entirely financed by the missions, and the lack of progress made by the Muslims is attributable to their lack of enthusiasm for western education, their lack of finance and of organization. In 1933 Bunyoro was the first district in Uganda to introduce an education tax, but as this was distributed on the basis of existing schools, the Church Missionary Society and the White Fathers' Mission both received five hundred pounds while Muslims only received twenty. Thus the Muslims were still left behind.[19]

Over the years the Muslims made efforts to build and to maintain schools but even as late as 1957 it was reported that the standard of supervision of the Muslim and Bunyoro Kingdom Government schools was poor whereas that of the Church of Uganda and Catholic schools was satisfactory.[20] Often Banyoro Muslims had to go to Buganda for their education, but not many could do this because of the expense. Thus the progress of Islam in Bunyoro was handicapped by the poor standard and the scarcity of its schools which hindered the emergence of an educated Muslim community able to compete on equal terms with other Banyoro.

The election of Prince Aramanzane Mwirumubi as leader of the Banyoro Muslims does not appear to have had the same significance as that of Prince Nuhu Mbogo and Prince Badru Kakungulu in Buganda. This was partly because at that time Duhaga II was King and he was strongly influenced by the Protestant Missionaries. Duhaga died in 1924 and was succeeded by Winyi IV who had a more tolerant attitude towards different faiths. This then might have provided the opportunity for Aramanzane Mwirumubi to make his leadership effective but he was absent in Kaberamaido from 1929-1959 grazing cattle. As a result there was little effective leadership and the loosely organized Muslim groups in Bunyoro were in conflict over whether to choose another leader or to retain Aramanzane. The Hoima group under *Mwalimu* (religious teacher) Masoudi and some of the Masindi group were in favor of Aramanzane, but the Buhimba group under *Mwalimu* Omar Kanyabuzana and some other elements were not. The Hoima group succeeded in keeping Aramanzane and this was helped by his return to Bunyoro in 1959. Even so as President of the Bunyoro Muslim Association, he remained a figurehead.

In Bunyoro, as elsewhere in Uganda, the political parties in the early 1960s had religious affiliations: the Uganda Peoples' Congress with the Protestants and the Democratic Party with the Catholics. The Muslims supported the Uganda

be held responsible for his use of the material: Sheikh Ibrahim Bitamazire, Sheikh Twaha Ali, Ausi Rwakaikara, E. R. Muchwa, George Mpabaisi, Zaina Nyabatwa, Husein Barhwani, and Nyesi Zahura.

19   Annual Report Bunyoro District 1932: District Commissioner's Office, Fort Portal. Annual Report Northern Province 1933. District Commissioner's Office, Gulu.

20   Annual Report Bunyoro District 1957. District Commissioner's Office, Hoima.

Peoples' Congress. So when the Uganda Peoples' Congress formed the Bunyoro Kingdom Government in 1962 the *Katikiro* (Prime Minister) and two Ministers were Protestants and one Minister was a Muslim. The last, Ausi Rwakaikara, was in every way a suitable choice because he had had administrative experience as the supervisor of Muslim schools and as a member of the education and other committees. As a result of the 1967 Constitution the Bunyoro Kingdom was abolished and Bunyoro became a district. The assistant Secretary General chosen was a Muslim.

The foundation of the National Association for the Advancement of Muslims (N.A.A.M.) in 1965 was welcomed by certain elements in Bunyoro who no longer wanted leadership from Buganda. One Muslim group, led by Ausi Rwakaikara, with Sheikh Twaha Ali as the leading religious figure, favored the Bunyoro Muslim Association, becoming a branch of N.A.A.M. However, another group led by Sheikh Ibrahim Bitamazire wished to retain the administration and organization of the Bunyoro Muslim Association with N.A.A.M. acting merely in an advisory and religious capacity.

To summarize some of the difficulties Islam in Bunyoro has had to face: the lack of trained religious leaders in the past has had its profound effects. There have been most of the time too few Sheikhs, and they have had to work on a voluntary and hence part-time basis. The Banyoro by tradition did not mutilate the body and so the idea of circumcision was repugnant to them. On the other hand, though this in the past may have prevented proselytism, these days it is less of an objection. Islam, being non-western and having a liberal attitude to polygymy has much to commend itself to the Banyoro. Islam has had to face intense Christian competition. With British administration came the Protestant and Catholic missionaries in 1898 and 1902 respectively.[21] The people tended to follow the lead of the Omukama and his colleagues. Duhaga II who was a staunch Protestant, and his chiefs were all Christians. There were no Muslim chiefs. The Banyoro Muslims received little assistance from the Baganda Muslims and only since 1965 received help from N.A.A.M. Arab influence came indirectly by way of Buganda, and direct influence has been slight because only a few Arabs have settled in Bunyoro. The Asian Muslim community in Bunyoro consists mainly of Khoja Shia Ithna-asheri like the Kassem Mohamed family or Bohras like the Ebrahaimu Alliji family. They have helped, but have not joined in, with the Bunyoro Muslims. In other parts of Uganda it has been the Ismaili who have given the most financial and practical assistance to the African Muslims and there are only a few Ismaili in Bunyoro. Only three families of Asian Sunnis live in Bunyoro. These, like the Ismailis, have helped the African Muslims.

The Muslims in Bunyoro are (1968) administered by the Bunyoro Muslim Association, whose secretary has the responsibility of organizing the different groups in his spare time. In each center an association is formed which then

---

21   A. R. Tucker, *Eighteen Years in Uganda and East Africa*, II (London: Arnold, 1908) 172-173. Father Baudouin, personal communication.

elects a committee and once funds are raised a mosque is built. Such associations comprise a *Mwalimu,* Chairman, Secretary, Treasurer, and a Committee member with local responsibility for the area. Each local association sends two representatives to the general meetings of the Bunyoro Muslim Association. Excellent work is being done at the local level, so one can with confidence look forward to a good future for Islam in Bunyoro.

5.   ANKOLE, TORO, AND KIGEZI

Ankole is the district to the southwest of Uganda which was brought together for administrative purposes by the British around the nucleus of the old Kingdom of Nkore.[22] The population at the end of the colonial period was probably less than three-quarters of a million. Less than two percent of this were Muslim, about twenty-four percent were Protestant, and thirty percent Catholic.

Islam was originally brought by Swahili and Arab traders who, however, left little permanent mark. After the civil wars in Buganda had died down, men who had been converted to Islam in Kabaka Mutesa's day or at Kijungute when the Muslim Kabaka Kalema was holding out against the Christians came to Ankole and settled there. For instance, Zaidi Kauzi was a Munyoro converted by the Baganda at Kijungute. He tried to settle in Buganda after the death of Kabaka Kalema but the new civil war under Mwanga went unfavorably to the Muslims, and in the 1890s he escaped with a group of followers and began a new life in Bukanga in Ankole.

The Entebbe Archives give us glimpses of some happenings in the next few years. When Kauzi died, Prince Mbogo sent a man to collect his possessions, but the local British official refused to let him.[23] In 1900 the new Muslim chief was killed, and the British brought in a Muganda, Abdul Affendi, but in 1907 they persuaded him to take the Bukanga area more completely into the Ankole sphere of influence.[24]

As the British began to organize their administration, a number of the other agents and Chiefs they used in Ankole were Muslims from Buganda. An outstanding person among these was Abdul Aziz Bulwada who rose to high office because of his friendship with the British and with King Ntare. It is said

22   On Ankole see especially K. Oberg, "The Kingdom of Ankole" in eds. M. Fortes and E. E. Evans-Pritchard, *African Political Systems* (London: International African Institute, 1966) and H. F. Morris, *A History of Ankole* (Kampala: East African Literature Bureau, 1962). Much of the material given in this section was collected by Jerome Bamunoba in 1964 and subsequently revised and expanded by him. Some of his research was published in *Dini na Mila,* 1, No. 2 (September, 1965), 5-17.

23   Collector R. B. Lacey to H. H. Johnston, 3 Oct 1900. Ankole Correspondence, vol. 1/21, A15.

24   Acting Collector Watson to Governor, 5 August 1907, S.M.P. 865/07.

that he had been a page at Mwanga's court and was under arrest for acting too arrogantly on the Kabaka's behalf. He was roped to one of the Christian martyrs when the latter suffered death by spearing, but lived to be released.[25] He became a Muslim in prison. When, in 1905, a British officer was killed in Ankole, Bulwada acted as interpreter at the trial of the suspects and was rewarded by being made Chief of Mitoma. He gave the Christians difficulties over the land on which they wanted to build but cooperated with them in eliminating divination and witchcraft. He behaved high-handedly towards the local people and was cruel to his wife. He was removed from office in 1908.[26]

As roads were opened up and the cattle industry developed, Muslims prospered as traders and meat-marketers and settled along the main routes especially at trading centers. They were sometimes called "the Jews of Ankole." But their numbers did not increase proportionately during colonial times, they remained under two percent of the population from 1911 when they reached that level till the census of 1959.

Muslim leaders interviewed in Ankole give various explanations for this state of affairs. The Banyankore used to detest circumcision even more than the Baganda. Becoming a Muslim made a man foreign, he had either to become a kind of Ganda rural Muslim or a Swahili trader-type Muslim, Ankole Islam was associated with outsiders. No prominent member of the royal family was converted. Islam tried to eliminate beer-drinking and drumming, both of which were important to social life in Ankole. The Muslims coming in were divided among themselves, they were traders not missionaries and could not offer schools and medical facilities in the way the Christians could.

From about 1945 onwards things began to go better for Islam in Ankole, overall numbers grew, though proportionately there was no increase because of the rapid rise in the population which is typical of the closing years of the British Empire in India and Africa. A good foundation for Islam had been laid and rapid advance lay ahead.

Toro was a kingdom in the west of Uganda which broke away from Bunyoro in the last century, was overrun by Kabarega's forces, then the Baganda, and in due time the British interfered and restored the kingdom. It survived till 1966.[27] According to the 1959 census the Muslims constituted two percent of the population. In the late 1960s this minority appeared active and important, if the well-packed mosques at Fort Portal, Kitumba, Bukwaare and Lake Katwe are taken as evidence.

The general sequence of events is fairly straightforward. The first meeting

25   *Musizi,* a Luganda magazine, June and July 1965. Article on Bulwadda.

26   Interview with Canon Yoweri Buningwire at Ibanda, January 1967.

27   This material is based on Abdu Kasozi's own personal knowledge. He lived
      in Toro for some years and had begun systematic research when he left
Uganda for California in September 1970.

with Islam was in the second part of the last century when Baganda war leaders and Swahili traders reached Toro. There was some influence from the Congo where Swahili traders and adventurers had made converts before King Leopold's authority was established.[28] These "Banyema" penetrated Toro in small numbers as warriors and traders, bringing some Islam with them. The Nubi followers of Emin Pasha and of the first British officers also contributed. For instance, we learn that in 1892 Reverend R. P. Ashe in Buganda sent some copies of the *Makeka* (first Christian reading book) to the Christians who were gathering around King Kasagama, but the Nubians seized these and burnt them.[29]

In colonial times, the country was opened up, and Muslim officials and traders brought Islam to the trading and administrative centers. Apparently only one of the great Chiefs inclined towards Islam. The Entebbe Archives show that in 1904 the Sekibobo of Toro became a Muslim, and a report was requested by Headquarters. The Sub-Commissioner replied that it was a true report but it did not indicate a general movement. He stated that the Chief concerned had fallen out with the Christians, owed money to some Muslim merchants and wanted to take an additional wife. Few prominent members of the royal family or great chiefs or members of the King's Council seem to have been attracted to Islam.[30]

We may conclude this glance at affairs in Toro by giving extracts from an interview with *Mwalimu* Hassan Kamihanda, who lives at Bukwaare near Fort Portal.[31]

Kasozi:
> You look an old man. When did you become a Muslim?

Kamihanda:
> Yes, I am very old. I saw Kabarega and Mwanga. I was circumcized by *Mwalimu* Hamedi, a Muganda in Buganda.

Kasozi:
> How did you go to Buganda?

---

28 See A. Abel, *Les Musulmans noirs de Maniema* (Brussels, 1960).

29 Oliver W. Furley, "Kasagama of Toro", *Uganda Journal* 25, No. 2 (1961), 190 ff.

30 Entebbe Archives, A14 vol. 3, 18 January 1904, reply dated 16 February. The list of Chiefs in Toro for 1906 (S.M.P. 559B 1906) reveals no Islamic names in the top group, six as against twenty-two Christian in the second group, eleven as against nearly four hundred Christian in the third group.

31 Interview on 6 June 1970 by Abdu Kasozi. The old man was said to be over a century old. Dr. M. Fitzgerald, a Jesuit who used to teach Islamics at Makerere, was also present. He is following up many aspects of Islam in East Africa and it is hoped that his researches will be published.

Kamihanda:
   I was captured by Mbogo's army which raided Toro.

Kasozi:
   How did you get back?

Kamihanda:
   Our King Kasagama went to Buganda and pleaded that since slavery had
   ended, all Batoro should be sent home.

[The old man then gave the names, so far as he could remember them, of
other Batoro who were captured at that time, of the first Batoro to become
Muslim, and of the first Nubi, Swahili, and Baganda Muslims to come to Toro.
One of the last was Aziz Abdalla.]

Kasozi:
   It seems Aziz Abdalla is ellhonored amongst Toro Muslims and colonial
   officials. What made him so well known?

Kamihanda:
   He came to Toro in 1930. His father was one of the Baganda Muslims
   who left home after their defeat and settled in Tanganyika. Aziz studied Islam
   there under an Arab, then he taught religion in Mbarara (Ankole), and
   eventually came to Fort Portal. He built mosques and Muslim schools all over
   Toro. The Omukama and the Europeans loved him very much. He died in
   1950.

Kigezi, the last area to be mentioned in this all-too-brief survey, lies in the
extreme southwest of Uganda where the borders of the Congo and Rwanda meet
Uganda. It is mountainous and heavily populated with peasant farmers who in
many respects resemble the Bairu of Ankole. Swahili and Arab traders came
there in small numbers in the 1880s.[32] Then in 1891 Emin Pasha visited,
bringing some Muslim *askaris* (soldiers). The British were slow to impose
effective colonial rule because of difficulties in demarcating the border with the
Belgians and because of stern and effective African resistance. By 1910 a good
number of British administrators with their accompanying Baganda and other
African sub-imperialists and their cooks, police, clerks, and storemen, some of
whom were Muslim, were taking up residence. As the routes were opened up
Indian Muslim and Swahili shopkeepers began trading along the roads and setting
up small market communities.[33]
   Islam in Kigezi did not spread as quickly as it did in Buganda. It did not

32   Information from Sheikh Hadad at Kampala in July 1966. For general
     background see M. M. Edel, *The Chiga of Western Uganda* (London and
New York: Oxford University Press, 1957).

33   Interview of Abdu Kasozi and Katherine J. Parry with Sheikh Habib Ibn
     Salim, 20 December 1968 at Kabale. Compare his interview with Hassan

convert an important and outward-going local group of people who would continue its work. It looks as if the local Traditional Religions managed to seal Islam off to be the religion of traders, travelers, transporters, and those living in commercial centers. In an agricultural country the men living in the fields were hardly reached. The Christians with their boarding school system drew the young out from the villages to their centers with the lure of western education and were able to give them Christian teaching. Much general and detailed research needs to be done on this area as well as the others mentioned in this chapter.

Ssebowa at Ndorwa, Kigezi on Easter Saturday (his dating), 1970, given above, and P. Ngorogoza, *Kigezi N'Abantu Baamwo* (Kampala: East African Literature Bureau, 1967), 5, 57, 62, 70, 85-86. On local chiefs and language, British policy wavered: Baziba (from Tanganyika) were brought in to replace Baganda in the 1920s and Swahili took Luganda's place. In the late 1920s British sought to replace foreign chiefs by Bachiga and to promote Luchiga. See also the *Annual Reports of the Western Province.*

CHAPTER IV

The "Presence" of Islam Among the Religions

1. THE YEARS SINCE INDEPENDENCE

The coming of Independence on 9 October 1962 did not immediately make much difference to the religious situation. This was in theory at least summed up on a postage stamp which was issued at the time. It showed the Protestant Cathedral on Nemirembe Hill, the Catholic on Rubaga, and Kibuli mosque, equal in size and on equal terms.

In matters of education the emergence of a national government with a strong desire to build nationhood over against all kinds of tribalism, sectionalism, and denominationalism, would lead to ensuring powerful central direction of schools and colleges. This inevitably meant that the religious bodies could not be allowed to exercise an absolute control in their own schools if they were to continue to receive state subsidies. In addition, there was a tremendous growth of facilities as a larger proportion of expanding national income was devoted to education. These resources would be used through direct Ministry of Education action, not through voluntary religious organizations. In this situation the churches would need more adjustment than the Muslim groups. The Christians had used their schools to provide education in general but also as one of their chief means of gaining new adherents and of imparting religious education. The Muslims had depended much more on attracting adults and imparting Islam to the young through the family and small informal groups. They had largely overcome their prejudices against "secular" education as such. They realized the new policy was of benefit to them.

In the matter of politics, the government of Dr. Milton Obote which was in power from 1962 till 1971 turned against the old kingdoms. In 1966 the Kabaka of Buganda was expelled and legislation for the abolition of the other kingdoms introduced. The trend of public statements was all towards the breaking down of tribal and traditional barriers and the building of a modern national state. The Church of Uganda (Anglican) faced a difficult situation for it had stood in a special relationship to the royal houses, also the Baganda were still providing a good part of its leadership and strength. This church was enabled to adjust to the new circumstances, partly because a number of leading Anglicans had as individuals been of service to Dr. Obote's party, the Uganda People's Congress. At one point that party was even given the nickname "United Protestants of Canterbury." The government also wisely chose to overlook the number of Anglicans who had been members of the *Kabaka Yekka*, "the Kabaka Alone."

49

The Catholics also adapted to the new situation. Some members of the Democratic Party (D.P.) including the first Prime Minister (Bendicto Kiwanuka, who constitutionally handed over power to Dr. Obote), were Catholics. The D.P. was nicknamed *Dini ya Papa*, "the Pope's religion." But many others had been found in the other parties, and it was rightly taken for granted by the government that they would be loyal citizens provided that no essential Christian values were contradicted.

It is not easy to sum up the position of the Muslims in this situation. Leadership had for a long time been in the hands of Prince Nuhu Mbogo and his son, Prince Badru Kakungulu. The Prince lived on Kibuli Hill at Kampala and worshipped in Kibuli Mosque. The colonial government in the best traditions of the Raj, and the East African Muslim Welfare Society, which had been founded by the Aga Khan, both found it fitting to work with and through the Prince and his people at Kibuli. In one sense the Prince was connected with the Kabaka as belonging to a collateral line, but in another he could stand separate from the Kabaka in that he had his own establishment as an aristocratic Lord of the land. Moreover, his was not "a Kingdom of this world" but a spiritual authority. It is true that the Baganda were prominent in the Kibuli circles, but in a national situation a man's territorial background should not be held against him if he is the best man for the job. The Kibuli people said that they truly represented the Islam of the nation.

At the same time there was a feeling, especially among Muslims from outside Buganda, that a new Uganda-wide organization based on democratic general meetings, elections, and publicly audited account-keeping should be set up. It happened that in Mecca in 1965 a World Muslim League organized a conference with representatives from many countries. The problem arose as to whether the leaders of the Ugandan pilgrims or the nominees of the Kibuli authorities were to represent Uganda. A promise was made that money would be sent to set up a League branch office in Kampala, but it was not easy to say whether this would be part of the Kibuli organization or form the nucleus of a new nation-wide group.

The events that had taken place at Mecca caused a considerable stir in Muslim circles in Uganda. At that time at least two Muslim gentlemen had risen high in Dr. Obote's government. One was Akbar A. Nekyon who came from Lango (he is said to have joined Islam as an adult) and Shaban Nkutu who belonged to the Busoga family we mentioned earlier on as joining Islam in the last century. As members of the government and as practicing Muslims, they played an important role in events, though it is not yet possible to define it clearly.

In August 1965 a general meeting was held and the title "National Association for the Advancement of Muslims" adopted. Office bearers to represent all parts of the country were elected. The aims of N.A.A.M. were proclaimed as:

1.   To find means and ways of paying religious teachers.

2. To cooperate with the government on matters related to the Islamic faith.
3. To control the collection and expenditure of Muslim finance.
4. To promote unity and brotherhood among Muslims.
5. To uplift the welfare of Muslim society educationally and economically.
6. To maintain a proper organization with a general meeting to be held at least once a year, the committee to meet not less than three times a year, and the officials to visit districts regularly.

Within a year N.A.A.M.'s influence spread all over Uganda. In Uganda there are about seven hundred main mosques, that is mosques from large ones like those of Kibuli and Wandegeya to county mosques like those of Butambala or Bugerere. N.A.A.M. spokesmen stated in 1966 that they had well over half these mosques under their complete command. The association claimed that it converted nearly two thousand people to Islam; of these half were in the Bukedi District. Their greatest support was, however, in West Nile in the Aringa area where about eighty percent of the local population is composed of Muslims.

In January 1971 General Idi Amin Dada took over the government of Uganda. The General is a practising Muslim. He is of West Nile background and was brought up among the Muslims of Bombo. In some of his early pronouncements he rebuked members of N.A.A.M. for mixing religion with politics but insisted that past mistakes must be forgiven and forgotten. He prayed the Id ('id) prayers in Kibuli in February 1971 and was photographed outside the mosque with Prince Badru and Abu Bakr Mayanja whom he appointed his first Minister of Education.[1] People are used to seeing photographs of the Ugandan Head of State after Divine Service outside the cathedral with the Archbishop. Islam, which appeared to have been put down in the 1890's, had lived to see a new day. We may now go back over the years and discuss her meeting with the other religions.

2. THE MEETING OF ISLAM WITH THE AFRICAN TRADITIONAL RELIGIONS

In taking the Traditional Religion of the Baganda as our paradigm for discussion we must not deceive ourselves that it reflects the general shape of anything like all the pre-Muslim, pre-Christian religions of the country. Thus on crossing the line between "bantu" and "nilotic" peoples which passes through Uganda north of Busoga and Buganda, we meet not only linguistic differences but changes of world view which have made a considerable difference to religion. However, the general features of the Ganda traditional system can serve as a basis for discussion and a general guide to the thinking of the people of the old kingdoms of Ankole, Bunyoro and Toro, and parts of Busoga.

Islam came before Christianity and bore the brunt of the first impact. In the kingdoms the monarchs held a position which is not easy to define. They

1 Reported in *The People* (a Kampala newspaper) on 8 February 1971.

"personed forth" the kingdom, they had "eaten" the country, they *were* that people; all power, all life flowed into and out from them. They could contend with the gods and spirits, punishing their representatives, raiding their estates, playing one off against another. So far as the clan spirits and the spirits of the ancestors were concerned, the Kings had to respect them but they could exercise power over against the clan heads and manipulate clan members especially off the localities where the family and clan spirits could protect their own people.

Islam of an Arab and Sunni background has long experience of dealing with sacral monarchy. It may appear to compromise but contains within itself elements which soon attempt to subjugate the monarch to the sacred law and in the long run may insist on the leadership being given to the best and most pious persons irrespective of their descent. It can be contended that it was this clash between Islam and sacral monarch which in the last resort caused Mutesa's persecution of Islam. However, the King had waited too long and Islam was too strong.

It was the Muslims too who first met the local African systems of gods and spirits. In Buganda these are called the *balubaale*. Katonda is recognized today by Muslims and Christians alike as "Allah" or "the God and Father of our Lord Jesus Christ." But if one studies the *balubaale* carefully it becomes apparent that in some traditions Mukasa the Lord of the Lake had most attention paid to him as a kind of supreme god, while Katonda was a shadowy and little known creator-god. Though it would be nearly impossible now after over a century of Muslim and Christian influence to prove (or, for that matter, disprove), it is reasonable to suggest for academic discussion that it was Muslims or Baganda reacting to Islam who aligned Katonda with God and the Christians who took up the idea.

In Bunyoro and the Western Kingdoms the *bacwezi* are a group of spirits similar in some respects to the *balubaale,* but they are much more evidently deified heroes and great leaders of the past. The supreme God, Ruhanga, is in some traditions counted amongst them but in others exists transcendently and apart. Muslims and Christians accept him as being a foreshadowing of their God and a place of common ground with the Traditional Religion from which they can start.

The Christians ran into difficulties in Acholi (which is outside the "bantu" area) by trying to use the methods and ideas they had picked up in Buganda. The Acholi do not appear to have a clear belief in a supreme God and creator, though they see the universe as being spirit-indwelt and this power manifest in various *jogi* (singular *jok*).[2] Some tried to import a European word, "Dio," for God; others used the Runyoro "Ruhanga." Unfortunately, this was closely

---

2   See J. K. Russell, *Men Without God?* (London:Highway Press, 1966) and
     J. p'Bitek Okot, "The Concept of *Jok* Among the Acholi and Lango",
Uganda Journal, 27 (1963), 15-29. Knowing Okot's sense of humor, it may yet
prove to be a solemn academic jape.

aligned by some with *Jok Rubanga* who was especially responsible for tuberculosis of the spine. Research so far does not enable us to say for sure how Islam dealt with this in Acholi. The incomplete evidence available would suggest the Muslims avoided this problem by using the Luganda "Katonda" or the Arabic "Allah."

Another area in which Islam came into some measure of conflict and yet of congruence with traditional beliefs and practices was in regard to marriage and the status of women. In traditional society a rich and powerful man could have any number of wives; their rights were those of the families from which they had come and of which they were in some sense still members. Senior women of the family or group had great authority, especially over women who had not yet brought forth children. Islam insisted on the rights of woman; she was to inherit a share, she was to be legally married by the use of the idea of contract - as long as she fulfilled her part of it, she had rights. The grounds and manner of divorce were carefully laid down. Clearly Islam and Traditional Religion would take time to adjust, but would not come into the headlong clash produced by the Christian ideal of monogynous permanent marriage and rare divorce reluctantly granted, if at all.

Some of the other features of the meeting of Islam with traditional customs will be apparent from the following verbatim extract from a long series of discussions which took place in 1966 with Sheikh Shuaib Ssemakula:[3]

King:
How about the installing of the heir and the ending of mourning?

Ssemakula:
For a Muslim it is important not to delay burial, but to wash the body, wrap it properly, and bury it with proper prayers. According to custom there was delay in burial and the mourners did not wash while they waited. We are partly sympathetic but only exempt people close to the dead from the prayers and their ablutions. We strongly disapprove of any sexual immorality in connection with mourning. We disapprove of the tradition by which a clan head could give all the property to one son whom he favored. We prefer to see the property distributed among the children including the daughters within three days of death.

King:
What is your attitude to the naming of children after ancestors and the special ceremonies for twins?

Ssemakula:
We like to give children Muslim names and disapprove of tests of legitimacy such as seeing whether umbilical cords float. In the case of naming twins there was a big ceremony in which the twins were objects of veneration.

3   The extract is from a recording made on 26 October 1965. The conversation was in Kiswahili. The translation is by Martin Mbwana. The Ganda traditions referred to are studied in detail in King's *Religions of Africa*, 65 and 80 f.

Islam disapproves of this veneration, our attitude is that twins are a gift from God. Children are fruits from God. Sometimes he gives one child and others he gives two. Islam therefore would rather no special ceremonies were carried out on the birth of twins. If a Muslim carries out these ceremonies, we as Muslims shun him, we do not give him the greeting *Salam Aleikum,* [Arabic *al-salām 'alaikum*] we do not visit him when he is ill nor do we conduct the burial service when he dies. We shun him because he has abandoned the faith. According to Islam practice on the birth of a son one should kill two goats for a feast, and one goat in the case of a girl.

King:
        What is your attitude to the traditional doctors who claim the use of spirit powers?

Ssemakula:
        That is one of the issues that have been for me personally a center of controversy. Islamic law says that if a person claims power to foretell events his punishment should be death. The person who believes such prophesies is categorized among the unfaithful. This is because we believe that all occurrences are directed by God; it is he who wills what is to happen. Those who claim power to determine what is to happen engage in lying, motivated by desire to make money and to create hatred. I am disliked by some people because I refuse to associate with people involved in this practice. They say I turn my back on my traditions by not associating with them, whereas I rely on prayer to God. The practice was becoming widespread, it was carried on in all places where people gathered. I told them that this was belittling God and God would bring them hunger and poverty.

King:
        What is your attitude to traditional dancing and beer drinking? Some other faiths have had difficulties with this.

Ssemakula:
        Islam has had even greater difficulties. Other faiths do not forbid drinking alcohol which often goes hand in hand with dancing. Islam absolutely forbids dancing where there is drinking. Islam is against dances in dance halls. In Mecca there are no dance halls. Islam is now weak because of not coming out against things like dance halls. The only dances we approve of are the dances exhibiting the culture of the people. We entirely disapprove of dances that encourage sexual immorality and drunkenness. Dancing and singing by itself is a mere expression of joy and God does not disapprove, it is only when it is abused that it becomes forbidden.

Lastly, it may be noted that Islam was the first "book" religion to reach the East African inter-lacustrine basin. It confronted traditional society with the idea of writing and of a religion which anyone who could read, could set forth and be a leader.[4] The contention that the Muslims, far from being a conservative force, were the real revolutionaries, is not without force.

4   Allowing for the need to distinguish between Muslim and Arab, the nature of Muslim influence can to some extent be gauged by picking out Arabic-Swahili words which have passed into Luganda. Here are a few: *ssaawa,*

3.   THE MEETING OF ISLAM WITH CHRISTIANITY

The leading Sheikhs of Uganda say that their religion welcomed and welcomes Christianity as such, it is the form in which she came that they have found hard to tolerate. This can be expressed in various ways. It is possible to point out that, when the Catholics reached the country, it was the Muslims who encouraged the Kabaka to let them enter.[5] At the same time, before the Christians came, they had warned the Kabaka that the Christians were connected with people who would eat his country. This word had indeed proved true. In the same way in the wars of religion they fought against the Christians knowing that if the Christians were not resisted they would take over the country and foreign influences contrary to Islamic principles would be given free play. This fear too has been justified. When the *Bazungu* (Europeans) took over the government, the Muslims had to conform to their legitimate laws, but unlike the Christians, they could not rush forward to work with them nor to try all the new ways they brought. Naturally they also resented the injustice of the advantages the missionaries were given, especially in education.

This is something of the point of view of the Muslims who underwent the impact of Christianity. Looking at it in the context of the History of Religions, we see the deep significance of the remarks about the Christianity that came. It was not Nubian nor Coptic nor Ethiopian nor St. Thomas Christianity from India, but the Christianity of northwest Europe and of Canada and the U.S.A. The Protestants were mainly British of the evangelical variety, the Catholics were French, Dutch, French Canadian, American and British. Even the Verona Fathers were from North Italy and Austria. The external appearance this Christianity presented to the Muslim observer was one of restless aggressive energy and innovativeness. Moreover, these men came from nations which had carried chauvinism and secularism to great lengths. It was hard for them to disentangle elements in their own culture which were fundamentally contradictory to the Christian attitude, often enough they thrust forward Europeanness as Christianity.

hour, watch; *kitabo*, book; *Kalaani*, scribe, clerk; *kalamu,* pen; *kanzu*, shirt; *ssuwani*, plate; *ddini*, religion; *enjiri*, gospel; *ssaala*, set prayer, collect; *ssuula*, chapter; *nnabi*, prophet; *malayika*, angel; *mutume*, apostle, messenger; *ssabbuuni*, soap. Almost any page of R. A. Snoxall's *Luganda-English Dictionary*, (London: Oxford University Press, 1967) will reveal some such words.

5   The substance of the points made in this section comes out of long
     discussions with various Ugandan Sheikhs over a period of years but especially with Sheikhs Shuaib and Nsambu. On the welcome of the Catholics also see Gomotoka, *Makula*, 6, 2461, who names Choli as the spokesman for their entry. On Choli, see Stanley, *Through the Dark Continent*, 189. He was a Swahili who came in 1867 as cook to Khamis and stayed on to serve the Kabaka as a flag-hoister, gunsmith and warrior chief. He led an expedition to Toro. Apparently he had visited France in the Sultan of Zanzibar's service.

It is possible to discern something of the rhythm of the Muslim response. In the 1870s they were amongst those who originally received the Christians into the country; when in the late 1880s the various groups took to arms, the Muslims too fought. After they had laid down their arms in the 1890s they suffered from a period of stunned resentment, but gradually they found means for separate development. This turned out to be not on the basis of territoriality but in Muslims developing their own family life, habits of prayer and dress, and meetings in the mosque. They became suspicious of marriages with Christians. They tended also to take over certain professions and trades. Their education, outlook, and culture took on an Arabic aspect.

From this "place to feel at home" the Ugandan Muslim, as his confidence mounted, could reach out and select such parts of the outside world as he wanted. For instance, a good number of Muslims possess and read copies of the Bible in the vernacular. They interpret it according to the Muslim belief that the Jews and Christians have falsified their Scriptures, but the knowledge of the Bible possessed by many Ugandan Muslims would be the envy of many a young Christian. Similarly they have a deep knowledge of and respect for Jesus.

Perhaps because of the proximity of Ugandan Christians who emphasize western education, a highly trained and active ministry, and an apostolic succession of teaching connected with respectable parent bodies verified by martyrdom, Uganda Islam has certain aspects which are not found in Islam in many other places. Uganda Muslims are often able to tell you who were the people first circumcized in their district, who taught them, who were those killed for the faith, and who were the first Sheikhs. In talking to Sheikhs it often becomes apparent that they have been carefully trained and duly "enturbanned" by a senior Sheikh who has something of the aspects of apostle and bishop.[6]

On the Christian side it is possible to trace in some detail the attitude to Islam. This work has yet to be done thoroughly, but the following examples of material collected will indicate something of the way things have gone. Mackay, one of the first Protestants to enter Uganda, was a dour Scot who died in the African service. He was admired by the Muslims for his manliness and craftsman's skill. In November 1878 he wrote:

> I have made the faith of Islam a special subject of study of late and at every opportunity am able to put to confusion the pretensions of Arabs who represent the false prophet here.

On 10 August 1879 he wrote:

> By-and-by the king called us in. He seems just now in the humour for cross-questioning the Mohammedans. Last Friday he called Musudi (the one-eyed rogue) forward and posed him sorely on why they did not translate their Koran into other languages. We had a long and interesting discussion on

6 Muslim Ugandans speaking English seem to use "enturban" and "ordain" interchangeably. The Luganda is *kutikkira*, literally "to put on top of," and can be used in connection with crowning or putting someone in charge.

the Koran. I have found a tendency at times among the people to undervalue their own tongue and wish to learn English or Suahili, while I always endeavor to persuade them that their own language is beautiful and that they should all learn to read and write it and pray in it. The dogmatic statements of the Arabs are as ill-natured as they are follish and unreasonable, and I firmly believe Mtesa and the court laugh at them.

Today the king brought up the subject of wearing charms, etc. The Arabs asserted the saving power of pieces of the Koran being always worn on their person. I caused much laughter at their expense about this. Kyambalango took up the matter and, from his own experience, related many cases in which such charms did not make Mussulmans invulnerable.

They refused to believe that the Turks could be beaten by the Russians when the former carried the flag of Islam; but I mentioned an instance nearer home when the heathen Mirambo put the pious men of Unyanyembe to flight more than once. But a blind "believer" will talk much nonsense when he cannot talk sense.

On 17 September 1879 he wrote:

Went to court this morning, as I expected a renewal of yesterday's battle, being almost sure of there being a *baraza*, as last night the new moon was first visible. This closes the Ramadan fast of the Mohammedans, and they are particularly zealous just now. The half-breeds were strong in numbers and stormed, blasphemed and, above all, lied furiously. To the great amount of absurdities they brought forward about the prosperity and power of Mussulman nations in the world, I replied nothing. I told the king that the religion of Jesus Christ was a thing quite apart from temporal power; that Jesus Christ was a poor man, and His religion was not one of the sword. Lourdel [the Catholic missionary] assented to this and, in fact, we stood fast together all through.

The Mohammedans railed on us as the worshippers of pictures, as having more gods than one and, above all, as being mainly intent on conquest. Mtesa began again about baptism. We would not baptize him, and he wanted an English wife and I would not give him one! He would not have me to teach any more unless I should get him a princess from Europe! I told him of the nature of such arrangements with us. "Peradventure the woman will not come." He was astonished when I said that no woman could be married without her consent. I brought forward the saying of our Lord, that "he that putteth away his wife and marrieth another committeth adultery." I received the very answer I expected - "I have no wife; my women are all slaves."[7]

Some extracts from the Entebbe Archives have been given above which indicate the views of some of the early colonial officials. The opinions of their

7   *A. M. Mackay by his Sister*, 104, 124-125, 128-129. Mirambo was an
      African King among the Nyamwezi of Tanganyika who was able to keep
both Arabs and Europeans at bay. See N. R. Bennett, *Mirambo of Tanzania*
(New York: Oxford University Press, 1971). A *baraza* is the holding of a meeting
of the court. Passages of equal interest from Mackay may be found on pages
127, 224, 225, 306, 320, 417, 446, 451. Mackay proposed a mission to Muscat
with the remark: "The Muscat Arab is a gentleman whom it is a pleasure to
meet."

missionary counterparts may be sought in such publications as *The Mengo Notes,* which were published by the resident members of the Church Missionary Society. In the number for May 1904, Reverend (later Bishop) J. J. Willis writes:

> The danger of a Mohammedan advance is one to be reckoned with, because even though the adherents of that faith in central Africa may know almost nothing of its teaching, and be scarcely if at all bound by its restrictions, once the heathen have become, even in name, Mohammedan, our great opportunity is passed, there is no longer an open mind.

In the August 1906 number he writes:

> That Mohammedan rivalry is something to be seriously considered must be patent to anyone who follows from a missionary standpoint the course of events in Africa.

He fears the "growing possibilities of a Mohammedan invasion of Uganda." He says Uganda is near Egypt and Islam might invade Uganda from that direction. He fears Islam from the coast:

> From the east, the railway has brought us into intimate association with the coastal influence; Swahilis and Arabs coming up the line leave Islamism in their wake, for almost every Moslem is more or less a missionary of his faith.

The Christians had to increase their work "if Christianity is to take the field successfully against the encroachments of Islam." Busoga was opening to trade and this meant an influx of Indians, Swahilis, etc. which will mean "a corresponding increase in Mohammedan influence. This influence must be combated before it is too late."

The missionaries did not fail to recognize the benefits the Muslims had brought - new crops, new skills, new methods of animal husbandry and trading, the opening up of routes - but they also believed in their Victorian evolutionary way that what they were bringing was of an even higher order and that there was a danger of the good preventing people from evolving towards the best.

The examples of Christian thought given so far have been culled from the Church of Uganda side. Similar material from the Catholic side is not lacking. Lourdel and other early White Fathers in the *Rubaga Diary* did not differ much in this matter from Mackay. Theirs was a society formed with Islam in mind. Again the Catholic Bishop Streicher's views, so far as one can ascertain them, were not unlike those of Bishop Willis. The Catholic Luganda newspaper *Munno* has carried pieces of material about Islam which grow friendlier and better informed as the years pass. Towards the end of the colonial period a White Father named Griffiths published *Where is the Truth?* which was used in Catholic schools to prove Islam a pack of lies. It is a comfort to find Martin Luther's desire for a wife being mentioned along with the Prophet Muhammad's admiration for womankind. This pamphlet was given the honor of being refuted by Sheikh Shuaib.

This kind of approach has become rarer. Father Franz Schildknecht, and more recently Michael Fitzgerald, as Catholic experts in Islam, have tried to educate their co-religionists in a more Christian approach to Muslims. In interviews Archbishops Kiwanuka and Nsubuga (in 1965 and 1968 respectively) spoke in understanding and friendly fashion regarding Islam.

In modern times Christian thinkers have come to appreciate more the many things they have in common with the Muslims and to recognize the service they have done and to for Christians in Uganda.[8] In a sense Islam was a *praeparatio evangelica,* for it made men familiar with the ideas of Adam (Man) and his fall, sin, forgiveness, resurrection, judgment, heaven and hell. Just as the Septuagint translation of the Hebrew Bible had prepared a vocabulary and thought-world in which Christian ideas could be expressed in the first century, so the teaching of the Muslims in the reigns of Suna and Mutesa made it easier for people like Mackay and Lourdel to be understood by people like Apolo Kagwa and Stanislaus Mugwanya.

The *Balokole* brethren, a movement within Protestant Christianity in Uganda, to reform it and keep it to strict Puritan ideals, to make Christianity a reality rather than the means of getting an education, are often most outspoken against Islam. Yet they appreciate the reverence strict Muslims have for the letter of their Bible, for praying regularly, for avoiding alcohol. They join in Muslim scorn for lax Christians who cannot keep to the women their religion allows.

On its side Christianity in Uganda has helped to produce an Islam which does not suffer from the false security and lack of vigor which monopoly can bring about. Ugandan Islam has learnt much from Christian mistakes especially with regard to laxity in the face of secularism and getting too close to the "powers that be." Muslims in Uganda have been made more aware of the need to keep up with modern education and technology and are doing so without compromising their faith. They have even received some fraternal help from Christians, for instance, in regard to broadcasting and television.

Increasingly in the last ten years Christians and Muslims in Uganda have come to see how much they owe to one another, how much they have in common and how much they can do together. This is much more positive than mere "Religious men of the world unite," for they hardly think in terms of "the secularist threat" and no red specters haunt their minds. The possibility of Muslim-Christian cooperation over matters of common concern has begun to open up exciting possibilities of mutual understanding. Thus both religions are concerned that the poor may be fed and sheltered, that the lot of those in prison may be alleviated, that there should be love and care for those to whom the blessing of sanity has been denied. Both religions put a premium on religious scholarship and humane learning, both desire peace in the hearts of men and in

8   Based on a series of conversations with Bishop Dunstan Nsubuga, Reverend Cyprian Bamwoze, and Reverend Jerome Bamunoba of the Church of Uganda, and Dr. Francis Mbazira, Father Byaruhanga and Dr. Aloysius Lugira of the Catholic Church.

the world. Both have to face violence, misuse of power, injustice, exploitation, secularization and the rape of God's good world. Till now they have hardly "met;" perhaps in the adventure of their getting to know and love one another lies some part of the best hope of their country.